Kirklees
COUNCIL

This book should be returned on or before the latest date stamped below. Fines are charges if the item is late.

D1493353

You may renew this loan for a further period by phone, personal visit or at www.kirklees.gov.uk/libraries, provided that the book is not required by another reader.

NO MORE THAN THREE RENEWALS ARE PERMITTED

DSRev12.6.2017

800532888

Ponds

Chris McLaren

Ponds

Creating and maintaining
ponds for wildlife

 THE NATIONAL TRUST

First published in the United Kingdom in 2009 by
National Trust Books
10 Southcombe Street
London W14 0RA

An imprint of Anova Books Company Ltd

Illustrations by Alan Hancocks

ISBN 9781905400751

A CIP catalogue for this book is available from the British Library.

15 14 13 12 10 09
10 9 8 7 6 5 4 3 2 1

Repro by Mission Productions Ltd, Hong Kong.
Printed and bound by WS Bookwell Oy, Finland.

This book can be ordered direct from the publisher at the website
www.anovabooks.com, or try your local bookshop. Also available at
National Trust shops.

CONTENTS

HISTORY

There is a picture of the quintessential English landscape that has at its heart a limpid pool, surrounded by rushy margins and set amidst lush meadows, where cattle come to drink and a small boy casts a worm in the hope of luring some monster fish from below. The air hums to the sound of damselfly and dragonfly and the croak of a frog pulses out from the water's edge. Swallows swoop at the thrum of insect life that masses above the water surface. Kingcup, water forget-me-not and purple loosestrife add bold swatches of colour to the scene.

Sadly, the British countryside has lost, over the past half-century or so, a very considerable and worrying number of ponds. To some extent 20th-century gravel extraction has mitigated these losses in the creation of new water bodies. But these flooded workings are generally large in size and the ecology that they support is often different from that of the traditional farm pond or flooded marl pit. This can be for a variety of reasons, ranging from the presence or absence of predatory fish to the different ways in which water heats and cools according to its mass.

WHAT IS A POND?

What constitutes a pond and marks it out from any other area of water? While there is no absolute answer to this question, the Pond Conservation Group defines a pond as being:

> *"A body of water, of man-made or natural origin, between one metre square and two hectares, which usually holds water for at least four months of the year."*

Our pond heritage is, to a great extent, the result of Man's activities – with natural ponds occurring much less commonly. It is also true that the recent destruction of so many ponds has been at the hand of Man.

So why did we dig them and why have we been filling them in? The most obvious purpose for ponds in the countryside has, since time immemorial, been for the watering of livestock and crops. Ponds were also designed as habitats for the provision of food: carp (or stew) ponds were a particular feature of the medieval landscape; attracting duck 'for the table' was another reason for pond building.

Others were created as the consequence of various industries, such as quarrying stone for building, collecting clay for pottery or cutting peat for fuel. In certain areas of the country ponds provided reed, willow and osier for thatching and weaving. Ponds were also dug in the form of moats for defensive purposes. As industrial mechanisation began to influence how the landscape was used, stored water was harnessed to power mill wheels for grinding and later for small-scale electricity production.

Ponds in all their forms have served as watering holes on highways, convenient places to interrogate the local witch population and as soaking pits for woodworking. Even bomb craters, left to nature, have developed into ponds. Not least, many ponds have been created purely for the pleasure of looking at them – from large features in managed parkland to smaller, more formal garden pools with fountains and other contrivances.

While all this human activity has been taking place, naturally occurring ponds have also formed throughout history – from oxbow lakes to the watery depressions left by fallen trees.

Apart from the physical characteristics of a pond, in any given landscape, the geology, the underlying topography and the soil-type all influence the various types of ponds as they develop and evolve. Clay soils hold water easily and the muddy waters of ponds dug into a clay base will be distinctly different from the clear water that will be found in a chalk pit (where water will tend to hold only as much as the water table allows it to). The biology of a pond will be as much determined by these aspects as it will be by it its geographical position, its profile, whether it is in shade or not, how unpolluted the water is, if the water is fed (from stream or spring) or if it rises and falls with rain and sun – and indeed by any number of factors. In short, no two ponds are the same.

Considered together though, ponds in all their shapes and forms support a vital and fascinating kaleidoscope of plants, insects and animals.

Sadly, with the advent of piped water supplies and the acceleration of modern farming and industrial practices, many of our ponds have become neglected, destroyed or have otherwise disappeared. It is the natural fate of all ponds to return to dry land over time and, even where this is not the case, the land in which they sit has often been (and continues to be) manually recovered for some other activity.

GARDEN PONDS

There is some encouragement to be had from the increasing enthusiasm of the general public for our natural heritage, and in the subsequent growth in support for wildlife charities, societies and trusts, such as the National Trust. Perhaps such groups will yet prove to be the saviour of many of our aqua-specific flora and fauna communities. Outside the organised pursuit of habitat improvement, gardeners are playing an increasingly important role in the preservation of many species by giving over dedicated areas of gardens to wildlife ponds and other habitats. Without gardeners finding space for a small area of water, the common frog might now be absent from large swathes of the country.

Frogs are, of course, among the star attractions of the pond, particularly for young children, and are often the prime motivation for wanting to create a pond in the garden – if for no other reason than improved slug control. Dragonflies, damselflies, water boatmen, pond skaters, newts and toads often help make up the main supporting cast, but more unfamiliar creatures such as the grass snake may also visit.

THINK BEFORE YOU DIG

While it is desirable that we recover our lost pond heritage by creating new ponds in the countryside, this must be undertaken with proper concern for how they fit into the greater landscape and the enhancement of local wildlife – as opposed to simply creating a new habitat at the cost of an existing habitat, which may be of greater value. Safety measures and any necessary planning and other consents must also be taken into account.

This short book aims to guide the reader who wishes to create or restore ponds for wildlife value for best effect and to offer help in maintaining the pond habitat as it matures and evolves.

CREATING AND
MAINTAINING A POND

Ponds come in all sorts of sizes and shapes, and with different purposes. The following guidance should apply to all but the most formal ponds or those that are intended for exotic fish, such as expensive Koi carp. For most gardens – and in the wider landscape – a new pond will almost certainly need to have visual appeal, be reasonably easy to maintain, be safe (especially where children are concerned) and hopefully attract a wide range of beneficial wildlife.

WHERE TO SITE A NEW WILDLIFE-FRIENDLY POND

The first question when considering the site of a new pond is 'Should the pond be created here at all?' If the site is in any way protected, or if its existing wildlife or historical value is of special interest or rarity then the answer must be 'No'. Next on the list is 'Does the work require any form of planning consent?' Other considerations include how to make the pond safe and the sources of water supply that will contribute to the pond's volume – avoid sites where pollution or nutrient run-off may be a problem.

In most gardens these are unlikely to be major issues. However, proper planning can make all the difference between owning a pond that is a delight to look at, easy to maintain and a haven for wildlife, and one that is murky, problematic and of limited wildlife appeal.

It's not essential, but existing suitable hollows in the landscape will provide sites that make for a more natural-looking pond – and may have the benefit of receiving a ready supply of rain water. On the other hand, it would be unwise to site a new pond in a frost pocket or in a hollow that is shaded by the surrounding landscape.

Leaving aside the particular attractions and specific habitat value of woodland pools, for a pond to be healthy it needs to have a good balance between light and shade. Light is required to promote aquatic plant growth, while shade subdues algae growth and provides shelter for underwater animal life. Translated into more straightforward language, smaller ponds are best situated at a little distance from trees or shrubs, allowing more sunlight to fall on the pond (and also to help keep leaf-fall out of the water). However, nearby trees and shrubs bring valuable protection from the wind. Larger ponds, on the other hand, will benefit from bank-side trees.

While any new pond will attract a variety of wildlife, those that are directly linked to good-quality, wildlife-friendly habitat will be colonised more quickly and by a greater diversity of creatures. If other ponds exist in the vicinity this process will happen even more quickly.

WATER

The most perfectly sited pond will be of little worth if the water that feeds it is polluted or high in nutrients. Water sources can be broken down into five major categories.

RAIN WATER

All surface freshwater has, at some point in its history, fallen as rain. In the British Isles this direct source of water is

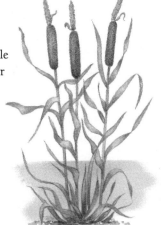

a fairly dependable one – although in some parts, especially in the south-east of England – annual precipitation levels are fairly low. To rely on falling rain to fill a pond may take an inordinate amount of time and so collected rainfall from water butts and the like is generally a good strategy. Bear in mind that rain may not always be a good source of pure water: acid levels (from industrial pollution) can sometimes be a major issue.

SURFACE WATER

When rain falls, much of it becomes absorbed into the surface soils and percolates down through the various strata of earths and rocks until it meets with, and becomes part of, the natural subterranean water table. Excess rain water floods off the land and enters watercourses, lakes and ponds using the most efficient routes available. Should these routes cross land that is heavily fertilised, or is otherwise polluted, then the water will become contaminated by elements that will be damaging or even lethal to animal and plant life.

GROUNDWATER

This often provides the purest source of water, as it is filtered by passing through the ground (often over long periods of time and over considerable distances). If a new pond is to be lined with a non-permeable barrier – as will be the case with most ponds – then it clearly should not be positioned where natural sources of groundwater, such as springs, erupt from the ground, or where the maximum level of the water table will lie above the maximum depth intended for the pond.

Streams mainly start their lives where artesian water sources reach the Earth's surface as springs. They eventually contribute to rivers as tributaries or become rivers themselves – direct rainfall and run-off from the surrounding landscape feeding this process. The quality of the water can vary considerably, with any pollutants present accumulating as the watercourse progresses downstream. Ponds that lie along a stream's or a river's course can be fed by occasional flooding or directly through tapping into the water flow. In both cases water quality must be considered and in the latter permissions and legalities may be an issue. Such sources can also carry suspended quantities of silts, that then settle in the still water of the pond, eventually reducing the pond's capacity or worse.

TAP WATER

One source of water that should be considered only as a last resort, when filling or topping up a pond, is tap water. There are two main reasons for this. In the first instance tap water usually has relatively high levels of phosphates and other 'nutrients', which promote the growth of algae and various undesirable, dominant species of plant life. Tap water is also an expensive commodity and in some parts of the country in sufficiently short supply to warrant regular hosepipe bans (including the use of tap water for filling and topping up ponds and other water features). If tap water is your only option then it is best practice to leave the pond unplanted for some weeks to allow the chemical content to burn off under the heat of the sun.

SIZE, SHAPE AND DEPTH

A new pond's ultimate size and shape will, to some extent, be determined by its immediate physical surroundings. Similarly, the ultimate depth of the pond may be limited by the geology of the site. As a general rule, the most valuable wildlife ponds are those that have an irregular shape and a range of depths.

If you have space for a larger pond, consider the value of creating a complex of ponds – all with distinctive characteristics – as opposed to one larger body of water. Not only can this look more attractive and support a greater range of plants and wildlife, but it can also help avoid some of the problems associated with large expanses, such as attracting undesirable numbers of ducks and geese (which can quickly make ponds murky and less capable of supporting other species).

AT THE WATER'S EDGE

The pond's shoreline is a most important habitat in its own right. The more irregular a pond's shape, the more habitat you will create. The gently shelving and shallow water around a pond's edge is also the most affected by seasonal water levels and is known as the 'drawdown zone'. The occasional drying out and re-hydrating of the pond bed in the drawdown zone is absolutely vital to the survival of many invertebrates: the temptation to continually top up a pond during dry spells should be avoided. A reasonable area of shallow water around the pond's perimeter also has the benefit of being safer, not only for children but also for creatures such as hedgehogs, which may come to the pond's edge to drink and sometimes drown in more steeply shelving waters.

While a depth of less than 2.5cm (1in) or so in the shallowest areas of the pond will be important to its biology, it is equally important that there is sufficient depth elsewhere to ensure that animal (and certain plant) life can survive the colder months. Ideally, the pond should have some areas where there is a minimum of 1m (3ft) of water present in most months. This is essential where ponds are liable to icing up, as a shallow pond can quickly become oxygen deficient when sealed by ice and may even freeze solid. Best of all are ponds with a variety of different depths created by an uneven pond bed.

Thought should also be given to the composition of the pond bed. It is ideal to have variety, with areas of thick, soft mud and others where gravels or harder surfaces predominate. Both hard and soft bottoms will have different purposes and value for a wide variety of invertebrates, amphibians and fish.

CONSTRUCTION AND MATERIALS

Your first consideration should be that any work avoids disturbing nesting or hibernating wildlife on or near the site. Time should also be allowed for any chemical content in the water to burn off prior to stocking the pond and due regard given to the best time for planting up (see page 20). The temperature and moisture content of the soil is well worth giving thought to before picking up a spade.

DIGGING OUT

Soil that is too cold can be hard to dig; if it is too dry it can be difficult to shape, and where it is too wet you may find it impossible to make much progress at all. These same problems apply if using hired machinery. Large digging machines may sink in the ground around the site (or damage the land they cross to reach the site), but smaller mini-diggers can make short work of an otherwise tough task. It is wise to dig the pond out fractionally deeper than the eventual depth required, to allow for sedimentation, thickness of underlay, and so on.

The disposal of spoil must also be taken into account. If this is to be disposed of off-site then appropriate permissions must be sought. In larger ponds, spoil can be used to create islands, although care should be taken to ensure that the richer topsoil is kept out of the water where it may create nutrient problems. Smaller volumes of spoil can be used to create mounds and other features that provide shelter – but again, don't site these too close to the pond, as nutrients may run off and enter the water.

POND LININGS

Pond linings come in a variety of types and, as with most things, the more you invest in quality materials, the more satisfactory and long-lasting the final product will be. Of course, the pond's size may be a determining factor here, with the largest ponds requiring particular thought with regard to the balance between cost and end result.

Pre-formed plastic or glass-fibre ponds are both cheap and easily sourced – garden centres usually stock them in abundance. However, these types of pond are best avoided as they do not generally provide a sufficient drawdown zone and it is often difficult to dig a hole to fit the unit precisely. The steep shelf edges do not allow soils to adhere to them, making the pre-formed pond less useful to animal and plant life and making it difficult to disguise the unit's unattractive construction material.

Concrete can be used to line a pond but chemicals in the mix can prove problematic and leaks can be difficult to trace and mend.

Polythene liners, being flexible, are a much easier (and cheaper) option but these can need replacing after a number of years and, where exposed to the sun along the pond edge, can quickly degrade and crack.

Butyl rubber liners are a far better alternative to all of the above, being entirely flexible, having a long life (the better-quality products often carrying lifetime guarantees), being easily repaired and manufactured to sizes suitable for even the largest ponds (in fact butyl is often used to line reservoirs, where large sheets are secured together using waterproof tapes). It also has the advantage of providing a surface to which soils can adhere and is more eco-friendly.

Puddling clays are an even better lining material for larger bodies of water, providing an entirely natural pond bed, ready for immediate planting up. There are various water-repelling clays suitable for pond lining, such as bentonite. However, the cost of transporting sufficient quantities – a good depth of clay is essential – can be prohibitive and the clay must be 'puddled' (trodden down) while still sufficiently damp, to ensure that it is watertight. Cracks can occur where the pond dries out and these can be difficult to repair. This work is best carried out by a professional contractor.

Anyone fortunate enough to have a good, deep, water-repellent clay in the ground in which the pond is to be built may find that a liner is unnecessary. Such ponds can be the most natural and biologically rich of all, but it should be determined that the pond can hold water throughout the year before adopting this approach. This may require a lengthy period of observation with regular checks to ensure that there are no breaches in the clay layer; that the clay layer is of sufficient depth; and that the clay does not dry out, in times of drought, losing water to any underlying permeable soils.

If you choose flexible (butyl or polythene) liner, then a good protective underlay should be considered. This will stop sharp stones and roots from puncturing the liner once it is under pressure from the water. Consider using this same underlay on top of the flexible liner. This will stop sharp objects on the pond bed from penetrating the liner and allow you to wade in the pond when carrying out maintenance. In addition, it provides a better surface for soils and gravels to adhere to. Many books and websites advocate using sand and/or old carpet to provide this protection, but these tend to be poor substitutes for a purpose-made protective underlay.

Butyl liners, polythene liners and protective underlay can all be purchased at garden and aquatic centres but online suppliers can often provide a wider variety of sizes (often made to measure) and better prices. Use the following calculation to estimate the size of the liner and underlay required:

Total length required = maximum length of pond *plus* twice maximum depth plus 1m (3ft) minimum (this last measurement to allow for edging).

Total width required = maximum width of pond *plus* twice maximum depth plus 1m (3ft) minimum (this last measurement to allow for edging).

LAYING THE LINER

Once the hole is dug, the floor of the pit should be checked to remove any sharp objects. Sand or screened spoil can be used to shape the profile of the hole further, creating bars, spits and other raised features.

Ensure that all edges of the pond are level with each other (if this is desired) by laying the timbers and spirit levels across various points of the pond outline. The protective underlay should then be laid down, ensuring that there is sufficient material overlapping the edges of the outline of the pond and that there is the minimum of creases and no air pockets.

The liner should then be laid adopting the same procedure as above. If using, the second layer of underlay can then be laid on top of the liner. Nutrient-poor soil (subsoil or specially prepared aquatic soil), gravel and selected stone can then be spread on the surface of the liner/underlay as desired. (Avoid using limestone or other 'soft' chippings or stone as these can leach nutrients into the water.)

The underlay and liner should then be lightly secured around the edges, allowing for movement when the weight of the water begins to take effect. The pond should be filled slowly to avoid disturbing any soil that has been distributed on the pond bed. Keep checking that there is no unnecessary strain on the liner and that the increasing weight of the water gently pulls down the edging of the liner so that all voids in the pond bed are completely filled.

Once the pond is full, the liner and underlay edges should be disguised by covering them with flat stones or, better still, by turfs that creep into the water. If you choose the latter, it is best to undercut the turf and add back around the pond perimeter, before laying the liner.

PLANTING UP

Before planting up, the pond water should be left for sufficient time to allow any nitrates and phosphates present to burn off (usually a few weeks) and for any filamentous algae to be eradicated (see control of blanketweed, below). If a truly natural pond is desired then no planting up need be done at all; most ponds will be naturally colonised by locally available species in due course. However, some of us may not be sufficiently patient to wait that long – and we may wish to create our own particular mix of aquatic plants.

Late spring is the most productive time for planting up ponds. By this point in the calendar the water will have warmed up and there will still be plenty of growing weather ahead to ensure the new plants establish properly.

Plants can be planted into any soils present in the pond, where this is deep enough to allow good rooting, or by using aquatic planting baskets. These plastic baskets are easily sourced and are constructed to allow water to permeate. Only properly prepared aquatic soil should be used, as this is sterile and low in nutrients. To stop the soil from leaking out, an inner lining of hessian should be used and, once the plant is in place, a layer of gravel added to top the soil.

When planning your planting, aim eventually to have around two-thirds to three-quarters of the pond vegetated, allowing some plant-free areas for wildlife that needs open water.

POND MANAGEMENT
AND MAINTENANCE

Wildlife ponds require little in the way of management once
they have found a natural balance. However, in the early
stages of a pond's existence some assistance can be given to
help establish clear water; later on a certain amount of weed
and plant control may be needed to maintain the natural
balance of the pond.

Before considering any form of maintenance, survey the
habitat and life present in and around the pond. Indeed, the
intentional or unintentional disturbance of certain species,
such as great crested newts, is unlawful and could result in
prosecution (see Law, Safety and Good Practice, page 89).
For large ponds and/or those that contain rare wildlife or
which are otherwise protected by legislation, ask a qualified
ecological research organisation for advice. In less sensitive
cases and in smaller ponds, the few maintenance jobs that
may need to be carried out can be done relatively simply –
taking care to ensure personal safety.

CONTROLLING BLANKETWEED

Filamentous algae (otherwise known as blanketweed) is a
common problem with new ponds, where nutrient levels
and a lack of surface shade combine to create the perfect
conditions. Where left unchecked, blanketweed can quickly
choke a pond, depriving it of oxygen, reducing light levels in
the water and inhibiting plant growth. Regular raking out can
help control but won't necessarily eradicate the problem.
Adding barley or lavender straw can help as these release
enzymes that act to moderate growth in blanketweed: it is

essential that the straw is only partly submerged for this treatment to be effective. Various proprietary biological additives can also used and, where properly applied, can be effective – but these have been known also to subdue the growth of pond plants.

To eliminate blanketweed, ensure that tap water is not used to top up ponds; reduce nutrient levels in the water, (such as excessive use of fish food) or indirectly (run-off from fertilised fields or flower beds); and make sure there is adequate floating plant cover.

VEGETATION MANAGEMENT

Removal of excessive plant growth may be necessary from time to time and this is best left until late autumn to avoid unnecessary disturbance to wildlife.

Submerged and surface plants may only require raking out (being careful not to damage any pond lining present); some marginal plants can be removed simply by pulling up; but others, such as irises with tough rhizomes, may need to be cut away. When removing plants by hand, wear strong waterproof gloves to protect against cuts and possible infection.

Removal of plants should not be excessive. Allow at least two-thirds of the pond to remain well vegetated and leave a varied structure of plant growth at different depths. Where plant material is removed, it should be left close to the pond edge for a day or so to allow invertebrates and other small creatures to return to the water. Never dispose of surplus plant materials by dumping them in natural ponds or streams.

Silting up should not be too much of a problem for most ponds unless they are fed by running water that is carrying sediments. However, the build-up of leaf litter and other items that may have fallen in the water will be an issue for most ponds over time. In the case of fallen leaves fouling the water, it is best to avoid the problem by netting over the pond in autumn – provided the pond size makes this practical and it does not endanger or restrict the movement of wildlife.

Suction devices (sludge pumps) can be employed to remove loose sediments from the pond bed, but these offer little control of what or how much is being removed – and you need a suitable holding area for the removed materials.

Hand-sieving can be more sensitive and allow for a more selective means of removing matter, but is not a practical solution for anything larger than the more modest sizes of pond.

Again, any materials removed should be allowed to sit near the pond edge for a while so that animal life can easily get back to the water.

TOPPING UP

As already mentioned, topping up pond levels may not be the best tactic where occasional drying out of the drawdown zone benefits pond wildlife. Where it is necessary, ensure that the water used is clean and free of chemical additives such as those often present in domestic water supplies.

In smaller ponds, long periods of ice cover can lead to the build up, beneath the ice, of methane and other poisonous gases (from the decomposition of plant matter and other such natural sources) and the depletion of oxygen in the water. This can be problematic, or even fatal, for free-swimming, dormant and hibernating animal life. The prevention of ice forming over the entire pond is preferable to breaking the ice once it has developed – as the sonic waves that radiate through the water from such action can also cause harm to underwater life. Free-floating objects, such as a child's ball, can help stop ice forming in small areas where movement occurs. However, exercise extreme caution where small children may be tempted to retrieve such objects.

PLANTS

*Left to its own devices, any area of permanent water will
sooner or later attract colonising plant life. Many species will
arrive courtesy of visiting birds and mammals, either by
seeds or living plant matter being caught up in the creature's
hair, feathers or feet, or by means of its droppings (where
seeds have been ingested). If marshy ground surrounds the
area in which a new pond is sited, then wet-loving plants
that are already present may spread to fill the water
margins. Others species – such as cottongrass – can be blown
in on the wind, where seed-heads are designed for the task.*

While this may be the preferred strategy for creating
a large wildlife pond in a natural setting and one
which blends visually and biologically with its immediate
surroundings, it is not necessarily what the gardener is looking
to achieve. In contrast to the lucky bag of naturally arriving
immigrants, the gardener is generally concerned with creating
something of beauty from a personally chosen selection of
plants, while still providing a natural haven for wild creatures.

Before considering which aquatic plant species to
introduce, thought must be given to the water's acidity or
alkalinity and to the nutrient levels that may naturally occur.
How acid or alkaline the water is may not be controllable,
given the geography, hydrology and geology associated with
the pond's site. Nutrient levels too may be hard to control if,
for example, run-off from nearby pasture is an issue.

Gardeners can often mitigate such problems by using
barriers and other tactics; equally they can create or
exacerbate nutrient problems by having ponds in close
proximity to fertilised flower or vegetable beds.

Responsible gardeners will also forgo the exotic pleasures of many imported water plants, as these may escape into the natural environment (see Alien Species, page 83) or be quite unsuited to supporting indigenous insects and animals.

Many garden centres offer good ranges of British aquatics but labelling can be problematic and the buyer cannot always be sure of the plant's origin. There are many good websites that guarantee that the plants supplied are nursery grown and have not been taken from the wild and are genetically pure in their British provenance. Even if you don't buy from these sites they are still worth looking at and will help you to become better informed. If collecting plants from the wild (and this is best avoided), then ensure that you are acting within the law, have the landowner's permission and are not endangering the plant's survival in its original site.

In this small guide, suggestions for planting are limited to those species which are either genuine natives or are long-established naturalised species that have proved beneficial or of no harm to the greater environment. A good field guide or appropriate website will provide greater detail.

TREES

In general, trees and small ponds – where some degree of water maintenance is required – are not great bedfellows. Fallen leaves, where they are allowed to accumulate, can foul the water and restrict what will grow and thrive there. The shade produced by nearby tree cover can also be problematic.

On the other hand, larger ponds and lakes are much the poorer for not having trees and shrubs around some of their banks at least. Leaf accretion is rarely an issue in large water bodies and indeed, where it does occur, provides a valuable habitat for many invertebrate species. Tree shade, being restricted to a relatively small area of larger ponds, can also be beneficial and will afford perching places for kingfishers and the like, and a ready larder of falling insect grubs for any fish present. Dead branches that drop into the water enrich the habitat by providing shelter, egg-laying opportunities and, where the fallen limb breaks the water's surface, drying places for emergent dragonflies and damselflies.

The following native trees and shrubs are suitable for planting with large ponds and other damp habitats.

ALDER (*Alnus glutinosa*)

Alders need damp or wet ground to flourish. Reaching 20m (65ft) in height they have grey-brown bark and broad, round leaves. Male catkins appear from late winter and are deep crimson. These are accompanied by female cone-like catkins, which may remain on the tree from the previous spring until late into the year. Alder wood will not rot under water.

ASPEN (*Populus tremula*)

A member of the poplar family but smaller in stature and relatively short-lived. Its Latin name refers to the way its leaves tremble in the wind. Flowering from February to May it bears fruiting catkins and has a smooth grey-brown bark. It was one of the first trees to return to Britain after the Ice Age.

CRACK WILLOW (*Salix fragilis*)

Similar in size, aspect and nature to white willow, with which it will often hybridise, the crack willow is so named because of mature trees' habit of cracking and collapsing under their own weight. For this reason they are often pollarded and ranks of them can be seen along rivers and lakesides where they help to stabilise banks and provide good habitats for small water creatures that find cover in the twisted, underwater roots.

GOAT WILLOW (*Salix caprea*)

A smaller native willow, rarely exceeding 15m (49ft) in height, bearing distinct oval leaves and, in older trees, deeply fissured bark. In January the 'pussy-willow' catkins appear which, by March, turn brilliant yellow and are very attractive to bees.

GUELDER ROSE (*Viburnum opulus*)

This member of the honeysuckle family prefers damp ground. It does not grow beyond 4m (13ft) in height. In June and July it sports pretty sprays of white flowers and later bears round, red and attractive berry-like fruits that are poisonous. The deeply lobed leaves turn scarlet in autumn.

WHITE POPLAR (*Populus alba*)

Growing up to 30m (98ft) in height, this deciduous, suckering and possibly native tree requires a fair area in which to spread and flourish. However, where this can be afforded it will reward the effort of planting, in time, with interesting bark, foliage and catkins but more so in spring months when young leaves and shoots bear a thick and most attractive coating of white down.

WHITE WILLOW (*Salix alba*)

One of our most familiar waterside trees, this large majestic native has long, elliptical leaves that, when young, are covered in fine, pale hairs (making the tree appear grey in colour). The bark is a dark grey and has rough ridges. Flowering takes place from April through to the end of May with the catkins being a soft yellow.

FLOWERING PLANT SPECIES

This guide is restricted by its size in giving comprehensive coverage of all the native aquatic plant species available. It focuses on those that are easily obtainable, are of most interest, are attractive and have most immediate wildlife value.

The division between marsh, marginal and shallow-water species is not completely definitive, and various species may thrive quite happily in all these particular zones. Plants are listed alphabetically by common name under each habitat.

MARSH AND GRASSLAND POND-EDGE PLANTS

Any pond will benefit both visually and in terms of wildlife value where it has a marshy or boggy area around at least part of it. Many of our most attractive wild flowering plants are to be found in wet ground and an adjacent area of marsh will provide a frame for the pond and an additional habitat to attract a wider range of wildlife. If it is not possible to have a marshy area, another natural option is to edge a pond with grassland that is left unmown for much of the year, where flowering plants can flourish and seed.

ADDER'S-TONGUE (*Ophioglossum vulgatum*)

A plant of dry grassland but often found in damp ground, this small fern is limited to the south of the country. In appearance it looks more like lords and ladies (*Arum maculatum*) than it does a conventional fern.

ANGELICA (*Angelica sylvestris*)

A tall, robust and handsome perennial with small pinkish or white flowers that form in a balled clusters and bloom from July through to October. It is not uncommon in Britain and smells very similar to its garden cousin.

BUGLE (*Ajuga reptans*)

Low growing with generally violet-blue flowers offset against oval, dark green, bronze-flushed leaves – see left and colour section for illustration. This grassland species also likes damp places and is relatively common in Britain; it can form wonderful sweeping carpets of plants. A perennial that flowers from April to June.

COMFREY (*Symphytum officinale*)

Flowers are bell-like and vary in colour from white to pink and purple-violet. A tall perennial with a natural habitat of damp areas throughout the country. In bloom from May to July.

COMMON FLEABANE (*Pulicaria dysenterica*)

From late July until September, this damp-loving perennial blooms across much of England and Wales where suitable habitat exists. The petals are yellow and set around a darker yellow mass of stamens in a daisy-like fashion.

COMMON VALERIAN (*Valeriana officinalis*)

Pale pink or white umbellate flowers form in almost rounded clusters from June to August. This tall plant favours the wet edges of ponds and ditches and is loved by bees.

COWSLIP (*Primula veris*)

One of our most recognised spring flowering plants, found across much of the country. Pale yellow flowers hang their heads from stems that emerge from a collar of bright green leaves. A perennial plant that prefers drier conditions.

COTTONGRASS (*Eriophorum angustifolium*)

Found in swamps and bogs with acid soils. The feathery white flowering heads of this wiry rush are delightful as they dance, en-masse, in a summer breeze.

CREEPING JENNY (*Lysimachia nummularia*)

Mainly restricted to the southern half of the British Isles, this plant is a low-growing, creeping perennial that sports yellow cup-shaped flowers from May to July. It enjoys damp places.

DEVIL'S BIT SCABIOUS (*Succisa pratensis*)

A common and widespread British perennial that is no less attractive for that. Flowers are lilac through to violet-blue (sometimes pink) and appear July to October. Likes damp habitats and will tolerate slightly acidic soils.

DOTTED LOOSESTRIFE (*Lysimachia punctata*)

Naturalised in this country. A yellow-flowering perennial species that will grow both in marshy land and shallow water. Flowers from June to August and is a good plant for bees.

GIPSYWORT (*Lycopus europaeus*)

A member of the thyme family, this nettle-like upright perennial has whorls of small, bell-like white flowers that appear speckled with purple. It is common in wet areas throughout England and Wales and flowers from July through to September.

GLOBEFLOWER (*Trollius europaeus*)

The flowers of this buttercup are sherbet yellow and appear as orbs of petals from May until August. A perennial that prefers damp places; it occurs throughout the British Isles and is widely cultivated as a garden plant. The plant is highly poisonous.

GREATER BIRDSFOOT OR TREFOIL (*Lotus uliginosus*)

A pretty creeping perennial plant with yellow flowers usually streaked with red that resemble a bird's claw – hence its popular name. A common grassland species that will happily inhabit and enhance the banks of most ponds. Flowers from June through to August.

GREAT BURNET (*Sanguisorba officinalis*)

Tallish with small, distinctive if dullish, blood-red flower heads. A perennial of damp habitats that is largely confined to England and Wales. Flowering begins in June and continues until the end of September.

GREATER SPEARWORT (*Ranunculus lingua*)

A species of marshy ground that will also grow in shallow water if it is sufficiently nutrient rich. It has glossy yellow flowers typical of the buttercup family though somewhat larger. Flowering takes place in June through to September. Found throughout the British Isles, although it is scarce in Scotland. It can be a vigorous species and should be planted with care.

GREATER WILLOWHERB (*Epilobium hirsutum*)

A quick-spreading and tall plant that often forms extensive colonies. Deep-pink flowers with white centres are produced from June to September. A species that needs full sun.

HEMP AGRIMONY (*Eupatorium cannabinum*)

Whitish-pink flowers appear, from July to September, atop this downy perennial. Plant in decent-sized clumps for best effect. A lover of damp ground and widespread in the wild.

LADY'S SMOCK (*Cardamine pratensis*)

An important food species for the larvae of the orange-tip butterfly. The lilac-white flowers of this damp-grassland plant appear through April to June. Prefers soils that are more acid than alkaline but the plant is common and widespread.

LESSER SPEARWORT (*Ranunculus flammula*)

A buttercup of wet habitats that flowers early in May and will last to the end of September.

MARSH-STEMMED ST JOHN'S WORT (*Hypericum elodes*)

Yellow flowers on rounded, greyish and hairy leaves make this an attractive perennial waterside plant. However, it will only thrive in acid soils. Flowers from June to September.

MARSH MALLOW (*Althaea officinalis*)

A tall, velvety and soft-grey foliaged plant with lilac-pink flowers that is relatively late blooming (August to September). It will grow in brackish marshes and still waters. See colour section for illustration.

MARSH WOUNDWORT (*Stachys palustris*)

Not dissimilar to a tall flowering nettle with whorled spikes of purple-pink flowers from June through to October. Relatively common throughout the British Isles. A favourite plant of bees.

MEADOWSWEET (*Filipendula ulmaria*)

Upright stems topped with foamy clusters of tiny, cream-coloured flowers distinguish this damp-loving perennial, as does the fragrance that gives it its common name. Flowers from June to September. Found in all parts of the British Isles and will tolerate slightly acidic soils.

PENNYROYAL (*Mentha pulegium*)

A short, downy mint with a pungent aroma that flowers from July to October. Dense whorls of lilac flowers mark this rare species that naturally occurs in damp and wet ground. See colour section for illustration.

PURPLE LOOSESTRIFE (*Lythrum salicaria*)

Bright red-purple flower heads grow from tall stems from June to August. Not usually found on acid soils and largely restricted to south of the Scottish border. An important source of nectar for many insects.

RAGGED ROBIN (*Lychnis flos-cuculi*)

Raggedy, dainty purple-pink flowers identify this charming plant of damp places. Flowers occur in May to July and are important to insect species including butterflies.

REED SWEET-GRASS (*Glyceria maxima*)

A tall waterside grass that has bright green, shiny leaves on stems that terminate in a multi-flowered spikelet.

Skullcap (*Scutellaria lateriflora*)

A generally short and creeping perennial with attractive violet-blue flowers that appear in June and can last through until September. Likes sunny spots in damp conditions but dislikes acid soils.

Sneezewort (*Achillea ptarmica*)

Grows throughout the British Isles on acid or neutral damp soils. A rather tall and hairy perennial with greyish leaves and white flower heads. Flowers from July to September.

Soft rush (*Juncus effusus*)

A familiar rush of boggy ground. Its glossy, dark green stems hold little tufts of brown flowers a few inches from the top.

Square-stalked St John's wort (*Hypericum tetrapterum*)

A perennial plant of variable height, with pale yellow flowers and hairless light green leaves. The stems are square, hence the common name. Flowers from June through to September.

Tufted loosestrife (*Lysimachia thyrsiflora*)

Restricted to Scotland and parts of North Yorkshire, where this tallish perennial can be found growing in pond edges as well as in damp habitats. Yellow clusters of flowers appear in June and July.

Viviparous or common lizard (*Lacerta vivipara*)

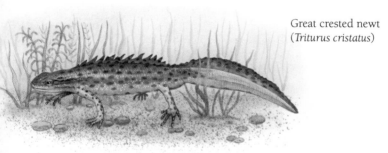

Great crested newt (*Triturus cristatus*)

Common frog (*Rana temporaria*)

Pike
(*Esox lucius*)

Eel
(*Anguilla anguilla*)

Tench
(*Tinca tinca*)

Ten-spined stickleback
(*Pungitius pungitius*)

Broad-bodied chaser
(*Libellula depressa*)

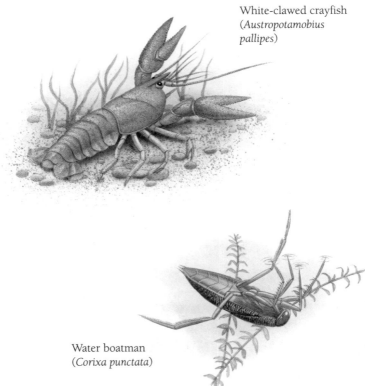

White-clawed crayfish
(*Austropotamobius
pallipes*)

Water boatman
(*Corixa punctata*)

Kingfisher
(*Alcedo atthis*)

Great crested grebe
(*Podiceps cristatus*)

Water rail
(*Rallus aquaticus*)

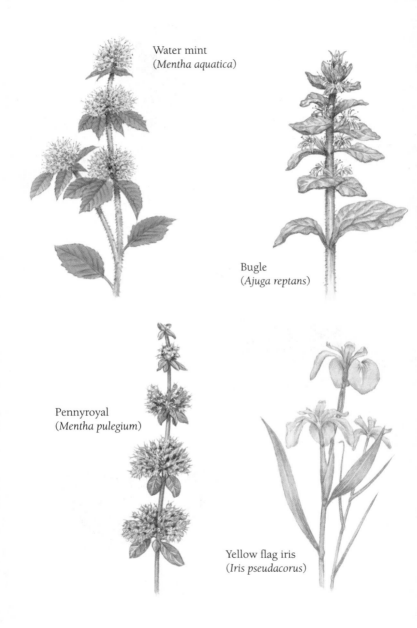

Water mint
(*Mentha aquatica*)

Bugle
(*Ajuga reptans*)

Pennyroyal
(*Mentha pulegium*)

Yellow flag iris
(*Iris pseudacorus*)

White water lily
(*Nymphaea alba*)

Marsh mallow
(*Althaea officinalis*)

Bulrush or greater
reedmace (*Typha latifolia*)

Daubenton's bat
(*Myotis daubentonii*)

Otter
(*Lutra lutra*)

American mink
(*Mustela vison*)

WATER AVENS (*Geum rivale*)

Cream through to pinkish nodding, bell-like flowers within a purple-brown calyx are produced from April to September. Prefers damp, shady places.

WATER BETONY OR WATER FIGWORT (*Scrophularia auriculata*)

A tall plant that produces purple-brown flowers from June to September. Fairly widespread in England but local or uncommon elsewhere in the British Isles.

YELLOW LOOSESTRIFE (*Lysimachia vulgaris*)

An attractive, generously flowered perennial with yellow blooms that last from July to August. Indigenous and found throughout much of the British Isles; generally a plant of pond, lake and river margins.

MARGINAL AND SHALLOW-WATER PLANTS

These can be described as species that like to have 'their feet in the water'; they grow in shallow waters and have either floating leaves and flowers, or stems, leaves and flowers that protrude from the water's surface. They have excellent wildlife value and provide food and shelter for many insects, fish, amphibians and birds. Aquatic grasses also provide egg-laying opportunities for newts, as does the submerged vegetation of many rushes and reeds for toads, fish and insects. Marginal plants bring colour to the pond and, with care, flowering can be planned to last from early spring until late autumn.

BROOKLIME (*Veronica beccabunga*)

A common and widespread marginal perennial that sports blue flowers of varying intensity, from May to September.

BOGBEAN (*Menyanthes trifoliata*)

Pink flowers, with white interiors, emerge from stalks below the surface in shallow waters from April to June.

BRANCHED BUR-REED (*Sparganium erectum*)

Male flower heads borne above spiky female fruits make this an attractive and rather unusual-looking plant. More common in the south than further north.

BULRUSH OR GREATER REEDMACE (*Typha latifolia*)

An unmistakable perennial, marginal aquatic with brown, sausage-like seed spikes that last through until February. See colour section for illustration.

COMMON CLUB-RUSH (*Scirpus lacustris*)

A very tall plant, with a spray of red-brown flowers forming at the top of the stems in summer months.

COMMON REED (*Phragmites australis*)

Suitable really only for large bodies of water, this grassy reed can quickly form big beds in still fresh waters.

COMMON WATER PLANTAIN
(*Alisma plantago-aquatica*)

Sprays of pretty white flowers emerge alongside attractive
elongated leaves from shallow water in June through to
September. Other indigenous and similar water plantains
include: ribbon-leaved water plantain (*Alisma gramineum*),
now a very rare plant in the wild; narrow-leaved water
plantain (*Alisma lanceolatum*); lesser water plantain (*Baldellia
ranunculoides*) and floating water plantain (*Luronium natans*).

GREAT FEN SEDGE (*Cladium mariscus*)

Otherwise known as saw sedge, this densely growing,
tall species has viciously serrated edges to the leaves. This
makes it a useful plant where you need to restrict access
to the pond margins.

LESSER BULRUSH OR LESSER REEDMACE
(*Typha angustifolia*)

Often found in marshes and ditches, this is a smaller relative
of bulrush.

LESSER WATER PARSNIP (*Berula erecta*)

An often-sprawling perennial with starbursts of tiny white
flower clusters carried on tall stems from July to September. It
is mainly only found in the southern half of the country and is
replaced, in parts, further north by the greater water parsnip
(*Sium latifolium*).

FLOWERING RUSH (*Butomus umbellatus*)

A small explosion of pink flowers erupts from the top of this perennial rush, from July until August.

MARE'S TAIL (*Hippurus vulgaris*)

A perennial water plant with erect unbranched stems bearing close, pale green whorls. Flowers are tiny and unnoteworthy. It can be a difficult plant to control once it gets hold.

MARSH MARIGOLD OR KINGCUP (*Caltha palustris*)

From March to April this cheery perennial with generous glossy yellow flowers brightens up many a pond margin. Much visited by insects.

MONKEY FLOWER (*Mimulus guttatus*)

Attractive yellow flowers, occurring July to September, are borne on hairless stalks that also bear irregularly toothed leaves. It is an uncommon plant generally only found in a few places in Northern England, Scotland and Wales. Blood-drop emlets or monkey musk (*Mimulus luteus*) is very similar in all respects to monkey flower except the flowers are spotted with red blotches.

PENDULOUS SEDGE (*Carex pendula*)

Tall and graceful with hanging flower spikes. This grassy plant has a somewhat scattered distribution in the British Isles.

STARFRUIT (*Damasonium alisma*)

The starfruit is now found only in a handful of ponds
in Buckinghamshire and just one in Surrey. The fruit is
star-shaped, hence the name, and it can only grow in
wet soil that is regularly churned to help it germinate.

SWEET FLAG (*Acorus calamus*)

A member of the Arum family, this iris-like perennial bears
tiny flowers in green-yellow cones. Occurs locally in the UK.

WATER FORGET-ME-NOT (*Myosotis palustris*)

This shallow-water species has pretty pale-blue flowers that
come into show from May until September. Its delicate form
enables it to blend well with other marginal plants.

WATER MINT (*Mentha aquatica*)

Strongly aromatic when crushed, the
lanceolate green leaves offset the lilac-pink
tufted flower heads to great effect throughout
the summer months. A common plant of
freshwater edges, it is present in suitable
habitats across the British Isles. See colour
section for illustration.

YELLOW FLAG IRIS (*Iris pseudacorus*)

Sword-shaped leaves and large bright yellow flowers
in June through to August. A common, widespread

and dramatic rhizomatous perennial that can be difficult to uproot if it spreads where it's not wanted. See previous page and colour section for illustration.

SUBMERGED OXYGENATING PLANTS AND FLOATING-LEAVED PLANTS

These are essential to the health of any pond, providing the water with oxygen and subduing algae at the same time. They also provide necessary shade and cover and a good underwater habitat for invertebrates, fish and amphibians to lay their eggs. Many are most attractive, with floating flowers as well as foliage.

BROAD-LEAVED PONDWEED (*Potamogeton natans*)

Broad elliptical floating and submerged leaves create good shelter for small water creatures. Flower spikes emerge in May and can last through until September. A good oxygenating species.

COMMON WATER CROWFOOT (*Ranunculus aquatilis*)

Attractive floating foliage and white flowers with a yellow cluster of stamens that blossom in April through to September. Prefers a hard pond bottom. There are a number of other similar sister species.

FROGBIT (*Hydrocharis morsus-ranae*)

Heart-shaped bronze-green leaves and white flowers make this a good introduction to any pond, not least because it is declining in the wild.

Rigid hornwort (*Ceratophyllum demersum*)

An exceptional oxygenator and good for pond life in general. Its feathery, submerged foliage is attractive but this species may need to be controlled as it can quickly choke ponds.

Spiked water milfoil (*Myriophyllum spicatum*)

Another good oxygenator with submerged and feathery foliage. The tips of the stems protrude above the water's surface bearing tiny flower spikes.

Watercress (*Nasturtium officinale*)

A familiar creeping and edible species (although the plant can host dangerous liver flukes) with white flowers borne from May and often lasting until October.

Water violet (*Hottonia palustris*)

From May to July, pale lilac flowers are held aloft on long, erect stems. The pinnate foliage remains submerged. It is common only in lowland England.

DEEP-WATER PLANTS

Deeper water species are more limited in number than their shallow-water companions but offer a dramatic effect rarely rivalled by species around the edges of a pond. Underwater stems and vegetation of deep-water plants offer shelter, food and egg-laying habitat for many fish and insects in what might otherwise be a somewhat sterile and hazardous environment.

ARROWHEAD (*Sagittaria sagittifolia*)

As suggested by its name, the emergent leaves of this dramatic plant are shaped like arrowheads. Flowers are white with a central purple blotch and appear in July and August. Although not native to Scotland, it is naturalised there and is indigenous elsewhere in the country.

LEAST WATER LILY (*Nuphar pumila*)

Similar but smaller in size to the yellow water lily (below), it flowers earlier and is generally found in nutrient-poor, acid and shallow waters. It is uncommon in the British Isles and is largely found only in the Scottish Highlands and parts of Shropshire.

WHITE WATER LILY (*Nymphaea alba*)

A plant only for larger ponds and lakes due to its great size. Its large white flowers can create dramatic displays from June through to the end of September. Plate-like floating leaves create shade and shelter for many aquatic creatures including larger fish species. Needs full sun. See colour section for illustration.

YELLOW WATER LILY (*Nuphar lutea*)

This is a more modest-sized water lily that holds its yellow flowers aloft on stalks from June through to September. Will tolerate shade although it prefers sun. Grows in water up to 5m (16ft) deep.

INVERTEBRATES

For a pond to support any higher life, it must contain a good 'soup' of microscopic creatures (some of which occupy that territory between plant and animal life). At the very bottom of this food chain are bacteria, single-celled organisms that form strands or spheres and that can only just be detected by extremely powerful magnifying devices. Above this level of life are cyanobacteria, barely any larger; spirochaetes and protozoa. While the individual cells of algae are themselves microscopic, they combine into the greenish, plant-like material with which we are familiar. Other life forms that require magnification to be seen include rotifers (wheel-like and free-swimming), gastrotrichs and bryozoans (colonies often look jelly-like). Moving up the chain, cnidarian colonies use tiny stinging tentacles to capture small water creatures.

As life starts to become more visible to the naked eye, common names begin to be attached to particular animals. Pond fairies (often transparent), slow-moving water bears, energetic water fleas and the appositely named cyclops all graze on the lower life forms described above and, in turn, provide nutrition for many of the larger invertebrate pond life with which we are more familiar.

These larger creatures provide much of the interest that draws humans, especially children, to freshwater of every kind – and no pond would be complete (or healthy) without them. The range of species that may be attracted to a pond can be considerable and many will arrive by flight. Others will turn up as eggs or adults, transported unwittingly by bird, animal or plant. Spiders will parachute in on silken threads, carried by the wind. Some, such as freshwater shrimp, appear as if by magic.

Related to lacewings, there are only two species representing this family in the British Isles. The alderfly (*Sialis lutaria*) is, in its larval stage, an aquatic carnivore best identified by the series of external feathery gills that run down the length of its body. It can be found in quite stagnant water among silt and decaying vegetation. Adults emerge from April and are often found resting on bank-side vegetation until August.

Spongefly larvae (*Sisyra* species) exit the water in autumn and spin cocoons in which they survive the winter, hidden in crevices around the pond edge. Pupation takes place in spring when adults emerge to lay eggs around May and June. Spongeflies are so-called because the larvae feed exclusively on freshwater sponges.

ARACHNIDS

These are essentially land-living creatures that include mites, ticks and spiders. However, there are two British spiders that associate closely with water, one of which is exclusively aquatic.

The water spider (*Argyroneta aquatica*) lives submerged for most of its life, occasionally coming to the surface to breathe. It spins an underwater nest in dense vegetation. It is common and widespread in the British Isles.

The raft spider (*Dolomedes fimbriatus*) is a large and impressive creature – a fully grown adult female typically being around 12cm (4¾in) as measured across the legs. It frequents marshy places and weedy ponds, and is now a very local and somewhat rare British species. The raft spider can submerge itself both to hunt and when alarmed. It is thought that its bite is mildly toxic to humans.

CADDISFLIES

There are more than 160 species of caddisfly in the British Isles, 71 of which are associated with ponds. The stony protective casings that the nymphs create around themselves are easily recognisable; inside the nymphs spin silken cocoons, within which they pupate. The adults are mainly nocturnal and have hairy wings.

CRAYFISH

Belonging to the same order as shrimps, our only native freshwater lobster – the white-clawed crayfish (*Austropotamobius pallipes*) – is now sadly an uncommon creature. See colour section for illustration. The introduced red signal crayfish (*Pacifastacus leniusculus*) now dominates many British rivers and streams, out-competing and spreading disease to its smaller cousin. Ponds are now important in offering some degree of refuge for our native species. The European crayfish (*Astacus astacus*) is also present in a broad swathe of Southern England, having also been introduced. While every effort should be taken to reverse the fortunes of our indigenous crayfish populations it must be noted that their habit of burrowing into the banks of ponds and streams can accelerate bank erosion.

DRAGONFLIES AND DAMSELFLIES

There are around 40 species of dragonfly and damselfly regularly found within the British Isles, all of which need fresh water for egg laying and for the nymph stage of their life cycle. Around 26 species are associated particularly with ponds. Adult dragonflies are conspicuous large insects and can travel long distances in search of suitable ponds in which to lay their eggs.

The two main groups of dragonflies are the darters – which rest on vegetation from which they launch predatory attacks on other flying insects – and hawkers, which do their hunting on the wing. Both groups can be distinguished from damselflies by the way they alight with their wings outspread; damselflies rest with wings folded along their bodies.

Damselflies are more delicate than dragonflies and their nymphs can be told apart from their larger cousins by having three tails. Dragonflies and damselflies have outsized eyes and hunt by vision as both nymphs and adults. Nymphs of all species are territorial and highly predatory, and the larger ones are capable of taking small fish. There is no chrysalis stage and, when ready to transform into adults, nymphs leave the water by climbing up on to vegetation or waterside rocks.

MAYFLIES

Mayflies are delicate, short-lived insects that are distinguished by their rather flimsy wings and by having two or three long and very slender tails. The nymphs can also be identified by the presence of these tails; the insect does not have a chrysalis stage. There are 19 species of mayfly associated with ponds in the British Isles and, despite their name, they can be found on the wing in all but the coldest months of the year. Most are largely nocturnal in habit.

There are, perhaps surprisingly, 34 species of mussels and snails that inhabit British ponds. In addition to providing interest, many of these molluscs do a useful job in helping to keep the pond clear of algae and dead plant tissue – although they can also damage living water plants.

The two most frequently encountered species are the great pond snail (*Lymnaea stagnalis*) and the great ramshorn snail (*Planorbarius corneus*). The great pond snail is the largest of a number of similar species and can be identified by its long shell (which is often coated in algae growth). Eggs are laid in gelatinous masses on the stems and leaves of various water plants.

The great ramshorn has a distinctive curled shell that can be quite red in colour but is more frequently dark reddish-brown. It can stay under water, delaying the need to come to the surface to breathe, for longer periods than most other water snails. There are other similar, but smaller, related species.

A number of British freshwater mussels can be found in ponds: the swan mussel (*Anodonta cygnea*) is the largest and often the commonest. It burrows in rich muds, filtering out microscopic organic particles on which it feeds.

SEGMENTED WORMS AND LEECHES

Segmented worms need no description. Most are aquatic, including marine species. Those that inhabit British freshwater ponds are represented by some 20 species of leech (some now rare) and eight species of flatworm.

Leeches survive by feeding on the blood of various animal hosts, including fish – a few species are capable of penetrating human skin. 'Medicinal' leeches have toothed mouthparts to pierce their hosts; 'fish' leeches have a form of hypodermic tube. Medicinal leeches are now rare in the wild. Leeches can reduce themselves to a jelly-like blob or extend their bodies to some considerable length.

Flatworms are related to tapeworms and flukes, but are not parasitic: they are mainly carnivorous. They can occur in considerable numbers and move with extended bodies, but will contort and contract when alarmed.

SHRIMPS AND SLATERS

Fairy shrimp (*Chirocephalus diaphanus*) inhabit temporary or newly created small ponds and pools where predators have not yet become established. Their extremely delicate and transparent eggs are extraordinarily resilient, remaining viable through long periods of virtual desiccation. A rather local and uncommon species, it can nevertheless become abundant in the right environment.

There are several species of true freshwater shrimp indigenous or introduced to British ponds. They are typically like small, greyish versions of marine shrimps and swim on their sides.

Water slaters and hog lice (various species) are common bottom-dwelling creatures that crawl through the debris on the floor of ponds and other still or slow-moving waters. They cannot swim.

STONEFLIES

Most of the stonefly species in the British Isles are strictly creatures of fast-flowing waters, with only seven to be found in still waters. For the most part highly secretive as adults, when found they can generally be distinguished from mayflies by having only two tails. As with mayflies there is no chrysalis stage.

TRUE FLIES

True flies only have one pair of functioning wings. Many are associated with still waters and many are biting insects, feeding on the blood of other animals including humans. Of these, various midge and mosquito species will be familiar to most people, but difficult to differentiate from each other. They do serve their purpose in the food chain: the larvae are part of the diet of underwater animal life such as the common bream, and adults on the wing are food for birds and bats.

WATER BEETLES

This large family of aquatic animals has around 170 species present in the British Isles. Of these the whirligig beetles may be the most familiar, being energetic surface swimmers and good divers when seeking food or safety. Whirligig beetles are often found in considerable numbers. There are around a dozen or so European species that live in ponds and one species that is associated exclusively with running water. The larvae are not dissimilar to small centipedes and generally frequent debris on the pond floor.

Screech beetles are so named because they can emit a rather loud squeaking noise if picked up or alarmed. There is only one species (*Hygrobia hermanni*) and it frequents muddy ponds, but is rather local in its distribution.

Diving beetles, of which there are more than 200 species, are often large and impressive and are voracious carnivores – both in their nymph and adult stages. The six species of great diving beetles are the largest, sometimes reaching 40mm (1.5in) in length, and are capable, as adults, of taking small fish and even frogs. Unfortunately, this genus is now uncommon in the British Isles – partly due to over-collecting.

WATER BUGS

There are about 45 water-bug species found in British ponds. Many do not have common names but among them are a number of familiar species.

Lesser water boatmen comprise the largest group. They are herbivores: various algae and organic waste material are their principal diet. Greater water boatmen (of which there are several species), on the other hand, are carnivorous creatures and will feed on insects, small fish and tadpoles.

Backswimmers look very similar to water boatmen but swim upside-down and are early colonisers of new ponds.

There are many common species of pondskaters, which 'skate' the water's surface in search of dead and dying insects that have fallen in the water and on which they feed.

The water scorpion (*Nepa cinerea*) is a common and fairly fearsome-looking beast with a flattened leaf-like body and long rear needle-like breathing tube.

The water stick insect (*Ranatra linearis*) also has a breathing tube that allows it to hunt below the water surface. It is a 'sit and wait' predator and has a southerly distribution.

Water measurers (various species) are slender, predatory bugs, widely distributed and common throughout the British Isles. They feed on water fleas and the like.

There are a number of British species of water crickets but these mainly occur in moving waters, although they will visit ponds on occasion. They are common and widely distributed.

FISH

If you think much of the beauty of a pond lies in its wildlife value, then think hard about introducing fish to the scene (although, of course, native fish are part of our wildlife heritage). As a rule, fish will diminish or eradicate the populations of many animal species by eating the eggs and young – including those of prime value and interest, such as frogs. Fish that feed on the bottom (especially carp) will uproot many water plants, stir up sediment and can leave a pond barren, muddy and otherwise unattractive – both to look at and as a habitat for creatures that rely on water plants for cover, food and breeding areas. Fish also excrete nutrients into the water and this can exacerbate or create the right conditions for algae to bloom.

On the other hand, a large pond that holds fish can attract terrestrial and avian wildlife that would otherwise be absent if the water were fish-free. The otter relies on fish as its main food source, as do some ducks, grebes and other wonderful birds such as kingfishers.

FISH POPULATIONS

There is a basic principle, if not entirely scientifically expressed here, that any given volume of water, together with the available food sources within it, will produce the same total weight of fish, regardless of individual fish size. Crudely put, this means that any particular pond might hold 100 fish of 500g (1lb) each or 1,000 fish each weighing 50g (2oz).

The average size of the fish present is largely governed by the availability of food, competition for that food and the presence, or absence, of predators. Any water containing predatory fish (such as pike) will have a reduced population of 'prey' fish (such as roach or rudd), but these 'prey' fish will tend to grow larger. By contrast, a similar water body with no predatory fish will tend to hold a greater population of 'prey' fish but these will average out at a smaller size.

Where the water holds only a single species of predatory fish, there needs to be sufficient young of their own kind present on which to feed to be able to maintain a population at all – a rare occurrence but this is the case in some Scottish lochs where only perch or pike may be present.

In small or modestly sized ponds, predatory fish are undesirable if the ideal is to have a good stock of other fish species. That said, a solitary pike in a larger, otherwise well-stocked pond may be beneficial in terms of keeping the 'genetic pool' healthy – predators tend to prey on the weak – and stopping a pond from becoming over-populated with stunted fish.

This argument can be extended to the entire animal life of a pond: the pond's 'biomass of life' relying on a healthy ratio of prey and predatory species. However, at this more micro level, a pond will generally find its own balance – just as a sparrowhawk, preying on the blue tits at the garden feeder, can only sustain itself while there is a population of blue tits to do so!

INTRODUCING FISH TO A POND

There are legal and practical considerations and responsibilities to be considered before introducing fish to a pond. The legal aspects are addressed elsewhere in this book (see page 89).

Practical considerations include safe (disease-free) sourcing and humane transport of stock. The pond should have proper provision for the fish, offering the right habitat for cover, feeding and breeding. The transfer of fish from holding tanks into the pond also needs to be carried out with some care as hypothermic shock can result if the difference in temperatures between the two water bodies is significant. Handling of fish should be kept to a minimum, as scale damage or the removal of protective slimes can expose fish to septic sores and disease.

FISH SPECIES

Fish are listed in alphabetical order and include native species and some introductions.

CARP (*Cyprinus carpio*)

Wild carp were introduced to the British Isles throughout the Middle Ages, primarily as a food fish. These original fish were smaller and not especially close to the appearance and size of today's monsters: carp in commercial fisheries, fed on a constant diet of high-protein baits and groundbaits, now scale up to 27kg (60lb) and continue to grow as time goes on. Carp are tough and cannot be described as pretty (especially the larger individuals); they have massive mouths in relation to their body size, with four barbules hanging from the lips.

Three distinct types exist, with variations in between: fully scaled, often called wildies; partly scaled, with large scales on an otherwise leathery skin giving them the name mirror carp; and with no scales at all, known as leather carp. To complete the look they come in a variety of colours and shades from bluish-grey to dirty-gold through to brown.

A muddy pond bottom is their preferred playground, where they search out a wide variety of food types including animals as large as crayfish. However, the vast part of their diet consists of smaller creatures: larvae, freshwater shrimps, insects, pond snails, worms and the like, in addition to seeds and fruits that find their way into the water. The method in which they search for food often causes waters to become muddy and depleted of plants.

Carp spawn at fairly high water temperatures, 17–20°C, meaning that breeding does not take place every year in our climate. This factor also restricts their distribution and few populations exist further north than the Scottish lowlands. A popular angler's fish, it is regularly stocked in many fisheries.

CHUB (*Leuciscus cephalus*)

The chub is principally a river fish but has been introduced into some still waters – mainly commercial fisheries. It is a powerful fish and may form small groups, but otherwise hunts alone or in pairs. Reaching more than 3.6kg (8lb) in weight, large chub are voracious eaters and will consume just about any plant or animal species that comes to their attention and can fit inside their huge mouths. Found throughout England (except apparently Cornwall), South Wales and southern Scotland. Chub are very long-lived fish, in some cases notching up 30 years.

A thick-set fish with a rounded head, flanks nearly the colour of whisky, pink-tinged fins and a tail of grey, it is a handsome specimen. Spawning takes place in April through to June.

COMMON BREAM (*Abramis brama*)

A large fish, sometimes reaching beyond 8kg (18lb) in suitable conditions. The bream is tolerant of relatively stagnant water and prefers a muddy pond bottom, although older fish tend to like gravel.

Bream is a bottom feeder; its diet comprises surprisingly small matter, including pond snails, bloodworms, insect larvae and various microscopic creatures in large volumes. It shoals in large numbers, patrolling still waters and slow-flowing river systems in an habitual pattern in the search for food. It is found throughout the lowlands of the British Isles but is uncommon north of the Scottish border (except where introduced for angling). The bream is a deep-bodied fish, narrow in profile and dark bronze on the flanks – although young fish are more silver and can be mistaken for the closely related silver bream (*Abramis bjoerkna* or *Blicca bjoerkna*) and various hybrids of bream, roach and rudd. May marks the start of bream spawning and when the water temperature reaches 12°C.

CRUCIAN CARP (*Carassius carassius*)

An introduced and most tenacious fish, the Crucian carp is characteristic of small, overgrown and poorly oxygenated ponds. Populations are often dense and fish can be stunted, but this depends on the availability of food. A fish of more than 2kg (4lb) is a prime specimen. Crucian carp are a dark, bronzy colour and have distinctive looks, but it is hard to determine the species' true status and distribution in the British Isles, as it readily hybridises with various other introduced carp species, making it quite uncommon in its pure form. The Crucian, however, does not sport barbules around the mouth and this may help identification. Diet is similar in nature to its larger cousin but, being smaller, it cannot deal with food items of the same large size. Crucians also need warm conditions to spawn, between May and August, and in the British Isles this may happen infrequently. It is a relatively long-lived species.

EEL (*Anguilla anguilla*)

The eel has a fascinating life story and has not yet yielded all its secrets. Most readers will know that adult eels migrate from freshwater ponds, rivers, lakes and canals throughout Europe to their spawning grounds in the Sargasso Sea (and perhaps now, it is thought, elsewhere too) and of the long return journey made by the young elvers. The adult eel is unmistakable: its elongated, dark, small-scaled, snake-like body marks it out as a powerful and solitary predator. The British rod-caught record for this fish currently stands at 5kg (11lb 2oz) but much larger individuals have been noted. See below and colour section for illustration.

Eels live in fresh still waters and feed on a wide range of fleshy prey – both live and dead. Small fish make up the greater part of the diet, but this is supplemented by a variety of terrestrial and aquatic worms, frogs, crayfish, molluscs, various larvae and fish eggs. Unfortunately numbers have declined in recent years, in part due to previous (and in some places ongoing) mass netting of returning elvers.

GUDGEON (*Gobio gobio*)

This small barbel-like fish is largely found in gravel-bottomed streams but can also be present in still waters. It rarely exceeds 14cm (5½in) in length and is a bottom feeder.

PERCH (*Perca fluviatilis*)

The vast majority of perch in any population are relatively small in size and readily shoal together. As they get older and larger there is a tendency for them to become exclusively predatory on other fish (often of their own species), when they can reach or exceed up to 2.3kg (5lb) in weight. These large individuals are, for the most part, solitary in habit. It is a most distinctive and handsome hump-backed species. Its somewhat roughly scaled skin is silver through to green with bold tiger stripes down its flanks; it has bright red fins – the dorsal fins are spiny and, when erect, can injure the unwary handler. It is large-eyed, as predators tend to be, and has a large mouth capable of taking good-sized prey. These include crayfish, worms, insect larvae and other fish, although young fish rely on a more microscopic diet.

Naturally found throughout England, the perch has also been successfully introduced across Scotland, Wales and Ireland. It requires shallow and calm marginal areas for spawning (at the relatively low water temperature of 7–8°C), laying its eggs among submerged plants.

PIKE (*Esox lucius*)

The British Isles' most impressive and effective predatory fish, the pike, is distributed throughout the British Isles except the

extreme south-west of England and northern Scotland. It
needs water that is neither high in acid nor poor in oxygen
and, for all its fearsome looks, is a rather delicate fish. The
pike is a 'sit and wait' predator that can exceed 18kg (40lb)
in weight – although all large specimens are female, with
males rarely getting close to double figures. Fins are slung
towards the rear of its long, lithe body and it has mottled and
often beautifully marked greenish flanks. The long snout and
large mouth armed with numerous sharp teeth make it
unmistakable. See colour section for illustration. These
features allow for fast and decisive action when an unfortunate
prey species happens by. Among the pike's range of prey, fish
feature top of the list, but it will also take frogs, ducklings and
other small animals where opportunity presents itself.

Pike are, for the most part, solitary but come together to
spawn during March and April in the shallow weedy margins
of still waters and slow-flowing rivers. Their lifespan tends to
be short but some individuals have been known to reach 15
years. A fish to consider carefully before introduction to a
pond, but with the useful function of removing unwanted
small fish and improving the average weight of prey species.

ROACH (*Rutilus rutilus*)

The roach is a very common fish and found throughout
England, Ireland, Wales and southern Scotland; it thrives in
freshwater rivers, lakes, canals and ponds. It is a shoal fish
that rarely exceeds 1.8kg (4lb) in weight. However, for all its
lack of size it is one of our most beautiful fish, being silvery
blue with striking orangey-red fins and a reddish eye. It is
catholic in its diet and will consume small invertebrates, algae
and waterweed, insect larvae, freshwater shrimps, pond snails

and much else. Spawning takes place between April and June, once the water temperature has reached a minimum of 10°C. The species prefers a clean, gravelly bottom for both spawning and feeding. Roach can be long-lived but are relatively slow-growing and, where conditions allow, will form large populations of small, stunted fish. Hybridisation with bream and rudd is common but the offspring are infertile.

RUDD (*Scardinius erythrophthalmus*)

Not dissimilar to the roach and arguably even more attractive, the rudd has warm golden flanks and a greenish back with brilliant red fins and gold eyes. Present in warm, shallow still waters and slower-flowing rivers from the south of England to southern Scotland, it also rarely grows above the 1.8kg (4lb) mark. It shares with the roach an inclination to shoal and has a very similar but rather broader diet. Rudd spawn on water plants from May to June and will readily hybridise with bream and roach. As with roach there is a tendency for populations to be stunted and, again, individual fish can live for many years.

TENCH (*Tincta tinca*)

This shy, largely solitary, bottom feeder prefers heavily weeded but otherwise shallow, sunny and muddy-floored waters. It will tolerate brackish water or ponds low in oxygen. In appearance it is smooth-skinned (with tiny scales), dark bronze-green, large-finned and is covered in a protective layer of slime. Description does not do this fish justice, as it is a handsome creature made mysterious by its small pure-red eyes and rather lugubrious look. See colour section for illustration.

Tench can be found in many still waters and in similar distribution to rudd. Their presence further north is restricted, in part, due to water temperatures needing to be at a minimum of 19–20°C before spawning can take place. Spawning occurs in June through to August but in colder years may not happen at all.

Molluscs, insect larvae and other small aquatic creatures constitute the bulk of its diet. Individual fish can reach up to 6.8kg (15lb) in weight and can be reasonably long-lived.

TEN-SPINED STICKLEBACK
(*Pungitius pungitius*)

Usually slightly smaller than the three-spined stickleback (below), and the number of dorsal spines present actually ranges from seven to twelve. It prefers still water and is fairly common throughout the British Isles. See colour section for illustration.

THREE-SPINED STICKLEBACK
(*Gasterosteus aculeatus*)

Its name well describes this handsome but diminutive shoaling fish that rarely exceeds 8cm (3in) in length. It is a common fish in flowing water but prefers still water and inhabits ponds of all sizes. In the breeding season it constructs a nest in the shallows. It feeds on microscopic animals.

WELS CATFISH (*Silurus glanis*)

A non-indigenous, massive, ugly, solitary, voracious and largely nocturnal predator, the wels catfish has been introduced into a number of English still waters. It feeds on fish, crayfish, amphibians, small mammals, ducklings, eels and much else that gets in its way, and is largely kept as a specimen species for specialist anglers. The wels rarely spawns below 20°C and so has little breeding success here. It will survive in poor water as long as there is sufficient food available. Ponds of a larger than average size, with soft bottoms, make a suitable habitat for this huge and potentially troublesome creature.

ZANDER (*Sander lucioperca*)

A recent introduction to British waters and a not altogether welcome one, the zander is a fierce and often large predator that breeds with great success. From original introductions in Cambridgeshire, it is now spreading rapidly through the river systems of the Midland counties of England and beyond. However, it is unlikely to be found in still waters except where deliberately introduced there. But still waters seem to suit zander and they quickly gain weight at the expense of the other fish populations. Of course, in time a balance between predator and prey occurs.

Fish up to 9kg (20lb) have been recorded in British waters and they can certainly grow to a considerably greater size than this. With a protruding head, massive mouth, large eyes and an impressive array of sharp teeth, the zander is not dissimilar to the pike. It also shares with the perch a rough texture to its skin and has spiked dorsal fins – earning it its popular name, the pike-perch. Murky waters are favoured in which it can more easily hunt down its principal prey of small silver fish. Spawning takes place in March and April. Zander do not live particularly long but they grow fast and are very productive breeders.

AMPHIBIANS
AND REPTILES

For many people and especially children, frogs are an
essential part of any pond's make-up. For the gardener, too,
the frog is a valuable addition to the environment as slugs
feature prominently in this amphibian's diet. Newts, while
less frequently encountered, are a fascinating addition to the
fauna of an area. Toads are less directly associated with
water but do, of course, need ponds and lakes to breed.
Reptiles do not need ponds for their survival but they can
often be found in the vicinity of ponds, where food sources
may be more plentiful. This is especially true of our largest
snake, the grass snake, which feeds on frogs and small fish.

All of these animals are mainly if not entirely terrestrial
and need good-quality pond-side habitat in which to
hunt and, in the case of reptiles, to breed and hibernate. Areas
of rough grassland, log piles, dry-stone walls, piles of dead
vegetation and sunny banks all contribute to a healthy
environment in which reptiles and amphibians can thrive.
Higher ground that is free from the risk of flooding and which
has soft soils for burrowing and/or fissures in rocky outcrops
is a vital habitat for overwintering reptiles.

For reptiles and amphibians in particular it is important
that ponds are situated within a greater landscape of other
ponds. Such animals are almost entirely dependent on their
own locomotion to colonise new sites and they can't travel
great distances. A complex of pond habitats is essential to
ensure that populations do not become isolated and subject
to increased pressures from predation and disease.

The introduction of alien animals increases the problems of pathogens affecting amphibian populations: common frog numbers have collapsed in some areas as a result – at the same time reducing grass snake numbers. For this reason and to ensure you stay within the law, never collect amphibians from the wild or from a friend's garden and add them to your pond. As long as there is suitable habitat nearby and no physical impediments (such as heavily built-up areas), they will colonise a new pond surprisingly quickly. Never add exotic amphibians or reptiles to your pond.

The animals listed below – frogs, toads, newts and reptiles – are all native to the British Isles. All of these animals are under threat and are subsequently protected by law to varying degrees. As a pond owner, whatever you can do to help secure or increase their numbers will make a valuable contribution to our native wildlife.

AMPHIBIANS

COMMON FROG (*Rana temporaria*)

The common frog requires little description (except to separate it from the other 'green frogs' that exist in the British Isles). This familiar amphibian can be very varied in size – up to around 8cm (3in) long – and more so in coloration. For the most part frogs exhibit a varying mix of olive brown with darker streaks and patches generally around the head and legs; see colour section for illustration. However, some individuals display more dramatic colouring being yellow through to orange and even pink!

Frogs are essentially terrestrial animals and use water largely for breeding and hibernation only – although they do need access to damp conditions throughout the year to keep their skins moist. For spawning a mere water-filled tractor rut can suffice, but a big increase in the number of garden ponds in recent years has provided the frog with possibly its most important breeding habitat – especially as ponds in the greater countryside have become increasingly polluted, degraded or filled in.

Breeding starts in early spring (and even earlier, on occasion, in the far south of the country) and this is when the common frog is at its most visible. The smaller males, which outnumber the females, conduct themselves in quite violent fashion in their attempts to mate successfully. Eggs are laid *en masse* but relatively few survive to become tadpoles and fewer still to froglet stage and adulthood. Froglets emerge from the water towards the end of summer and feed on a variety of small invertebrates, as do the adults. Hunting is largely a nocturnal practice and adult frogs will take many slugs, making them a friend of the gardener.

The common frog can be found throughout the British Isles and even at some height in mountainous country. The recent arrival of various fungal and bacterial infections has caused massive reductions in local frog populations in some areas, particularly in the south. In Great Britain and Northern Ireland, the common frog is protected from sale and trade in any form.

COMMON TOAD (*Bufo bufo*)

Common toads prefer deeper waters for breeding than frogs and this rules out many smaller and garden ponds. However, due to toxins exuded from their skin, toads can survive and thrive in waters containing fish species where frogs are prevented from any real breeding success. Large numbers of toads migrate to traditional breeding ponds and lakes in the early part of spring. Their spawn can be distinguished from the common frog's as it is produced in long, thin strings that are entangled among water weeds.

Toadlets emerge generally in August and roam very widely as adults. Common toads can be long-lived. In Great Britain the common toad is protected from sale and trade in any form.

GREAT CRESTED NEWT (*Triturus cristatus*)

A strictly protected species but widely distributed and in some locations often the most common newt present. Nevertheless, the great crested newt remains under threat in the British Isles and is absent from Ireland. See colour section for illustration.

Much larger – around 15cm (6in) – and heavier than other species, this newt will take larger items of invertebrate prey than other newts. It requires deeper water for breeding and is less frequently encountered in garden ponds. As with other newts, populations can disappear if they are reliant on a single breeding habitat that is remote from other suitable ponds. For healthy numbers to exist and survive in the long term, pond complexes supporting meta-populations are required. (Meta-populations consist of a number of discrete but inter-linked populations – for example, a complex of ponds, each with populations of a particular species, but close enough to allow migration, and therefore breeding, to take place between the various pond populations.) However, considerable numbers of animals can build up in suitable habitats – that is, areas of good, undisturbed hunting ground around the breeding waters. British and European law makes it an offence to kill, injure or capture, possess, sell, trade or disturb the animals. And it is an offence to damage or destroy their habitat.

NATTERJACK TOAD (*Epidalea calamita*)

The natterjack is an indigenous and now rare toad that is being re-introduced to some key locations in the British Isles. Currently it exists only in a small number of ponds mainly in the sand-dune systems and heaths around the coast of Merseyside. Previously it was more common, with colonies in East Anglia and south-east England. In large part its demise results from the destruction of the shallow, warm pond complexes it requires to breed in.

It is smaller than the common toad and has a distinctive yellow stripe running down the middle of the back. It has a loud and grating call that is issued, sometimes without respite, throughout the night during its breeding season, which runs from April through to July – its call is a key indicator of the presence of colonies.

Due to its threatened status the natterjack toad is strictly protected by British and European law, making it an offence to kill, injure or capture, possess, sell, trade or disturb the animals. It is an offence to damage or destroy their habitat.

PALMATE NEWT (*Lissotriton helveticus*)

Similar in appearance to the smooth newt (see below), the palmate newt is a rather smaller animal – reaching perhaps 6cm (2¼in) in length. An unspotted throat distinguishes the adult female from the smooth newt, while the breeding male has a less obvious crest and a filament extending from the tail, in contrast to his smooth newt counterpart. The palmate newt is widely distributed in the British Isles but less so than the smooth newt, preferring shallow and often brackish and more acid water, making it a less common animal in garden ponds. Breeding activity largely mirrors that of its cousin and its diet is much the same, but it can tolerate a drier environment and is not as reliant on pond habitat outside the breeding season. The palmate newt is protected in Great Britain from sale and trade in any form.

POOL FROG (*Pelophylax lessonae*)

Slightly larger than the common frog, the pool frog seems never to have had much more than a claw-hold in the British Isles (and is thought to be indigenous only by a narrow margin of scientific consideration). A small historical population in East Anglia finally became extinct towards the end of the 20th century and their presence here is now due to a few subsequent attempts to establish colonies in Norfolk and possibly a few private locations elsewhere.

Coloration is not dissimilar to the common frog, though tending more to brown, but individuals often have a light yellow stripe down the backbone and some have green heads. The smaller males make their presence felt in the breeding season with loud calls, created by inflating their vocal sacs that sit either side of the mouth. Spawning takes place in late spring, or even early summer, requiring warm conditions. Unlike the common frog, the froglets emerge the following spring – unless extremely hot weather allows this to occur towards the end of the summer. The species is not currently protected under British law but if the species becomes officially recognised as indigenous, full protection should follow.

SMOOTH OR COMMON NEWT (*Lissotriton vulgaris*)

Found in most parts of the British Isles, where it is the most common newt present, the smooth newt is primarily a creature of dry land, but ponds are necessary for breeding, which takes place between very early spring and mid-summer. Eggs are laid individually and are carefully wrapped in the tips of submerged broad-stemmed grasses or suitable water weeds. Efts (the newt tadpoles) remain in the pond until they fully metamorphose into adult newts. Adults can reach a length of around 10cm (4in) and the males develop a wavy crest along the back and become spotted during breeding.

Outside the breeding season the habitat around ponds remains important to newts, as they need damp conditions to hunt and survive. They are largely nocturnal hunters and take a variety of small invertebrates both as efts and as adults. While fish will eat newt eggs, the tables are turned when the efts hatch as they actively seek out fish eggs for food. Garden ponds have, in recent times, become a very important refuge for smooth newts and they are protected by law in Great Britain against being sold or traded in any way. In Northern Ireland the species are fully protected from the killing, injuring, disturbance, capturing, possession or trade of animals.

REPTILES

GRASS SNAKE (*Natrix natrix*)

The British Isles supports only three indigenous species of snake and the grass snake is the only one of these associated with ponds and water in general. It is only found in England and Wales where, while it enjoys a broad distribution in lowland areas, it has suffered substantial decline over recent decades. Individual female animals have been recorded at nearly 2m (6½ft) long, although adults more typically reach half this length. Their principal food is frogs and, to a lesser extent, fish – although they will take other animal prey.

Generally olive green in colour, most grass snakes have a distinctive yellow and black collar around the neck. Grass snakes will often visit garden ponds to hunt and can be seen swimming in pursuit of prey. They also make use of compost heaps for egg laying but cannot really be considered garden residents unless the garden is large and has a suitable habitat. Garden owners lucky enough to have grass snakes as visitors should be aware that they are harmless creatures (as are adders if left to their own devices) and every effort should be made to avoid harming them. Like other British reptiles, they hibernate in winter. They are fully protected by law in Great Britain and must not be killed, injured or sold or traded in any way.

SLOW WORM (*Anguis fragilis*)

Superficially like a small snake, this relatively common, indigenous and legless lizard can be found across the British Isles (including a small introduced colony in the west of Ireland). Although widespread, slow worms are both largely nocturnal and subterranean and are usually only found when overturning suitable refuges (such as dark, flat materials), under which they can often be found thermo-regulating – controlling their body temperature through their location. While slow worms don't use ponds directly, they often favour open habitats around ponds where they can find plenty of their favourite prey: small slugs. Hibernation occurs during the colder months of the year. Slow worms have protection in British law against being killed, injured or sold or traded in any way.

VIVIPAROUS OR COMMON LIZARD
(*Lacerta vivipara*)

Like the slow worm, the common lizard is not particularly associated with ponds. However, it often demonstrates a predilection for boggy ground and areas of high humidity and can be found near ponds in open and sunny situations – wet heathland being a particularly important habitat. It is a widespread species in the British Isles but rather patchy in its local distribution. Adults can reach up to 15cm (6in) long and they feed on various insects and spiders. The hibernation period varies across the country, but generally spans those months in which heavy frosts are likely. Common lizards are protected by law in Great Britain against being killed, injured or sold or traded in any way. In Northern Ireland they are fully protected, prohibiting the killing, injuring, capturing, disturbance, possession or trade of animals. See below and colour section for illustration.

BIRDS

Ponds are important to many species of birds for three
principal reasons. Firstly, ponds are a source of water for
drinking and bathing in. Secondly, ponds provide food, from
fish to amphibians, invertebrates and waterweeds. Thirdly,
for a much smaller range of species, the pond is a relatively
safe place around which to nest and raise young.
The size of a pond will have a direct bearing on the range of
species that use it. Generally speaking, the larger the pond the
more species it will attract – larger ponds offer a greater variety
of nesting opportunities and of prey species, especially fish.

For the most part birds are a desirable part of the greater
pond landscape, but some species can cause problems
and should be actively dissuaded from putting in an
appearance. Large numbers of geese and duck can cause
significant fouling of the water; the murky conditions then
inhibit aquatic plant growth and reduce the abundance of
invertebrates and biodiversity in general. Fish-eating species,
such as cormorant, grey heron and various duck and grebe,
can reduce fish numbers – although rarely to any serious
effect and often to the benefit of other pond residents.

Various benign tactics can be employed to reduce or
eliminate these issues:

- Planting shrubs and trees at a reasonable and sensible
  distance from the pond will affect duck and geese flight
  paths, making it difficult for them to land.
- Sedges, reeds and other tall waterside plants can deter
  herons, which can only enter the water by wading in.
- A lack of perching opportunities will usually restrict
  cormorant numbers.

However, in most cases the pond owner will want to attract a good range of species and these can be encouraged by including a variety of features:

- Shallow water and bare areas of mud will allow for wading birds and small perching species to feed.
- Deeper water give divers and ducks feeding opportunities.
- Overhanging tree branches make good perches for kingfishers to watch for small fish below.
- Decent-sized reed beds are essential for certain water birds to feed, breed and find cover in.

Although a larger body of water is necessary for many of the above-mentioned species, even the smallest pond will invite birds such as wagtails and thrushes to find food or bathe in. Similarly, the muddy margins of small ponds can supply valuable nest-building materials for martins, swallows and swifts.

While not exhaustive, the list below describes the more common visitors and residents of ponds great and small.

CANADA GOOSE (*Branta canadensis*)

An introduced species and generally not welcome on ponds where the birds can cause considerable water fouling. They are big noisy geese and use water for resting and roosting purposes only, but grassy pond margins become degraded when large numbers of grazing birds gather. Resident and generally common across the lowlands of the British Isles.

CETTI'S WARBLER (*Cettia cetti*)

A secretive bird that is more often heard than seen and has dramatically expanded its range in southern counties over recent years. Nevertheless it remains relatively rare and is likely to be encountered only around larger ponds with extensive reed beds.

COMMON SANDPIPER (*Actitis hypoleucos*)

This small wader breeds almost exclusively in highland areas of Britain, but will occasionally visit lowland ponds across the country during passage. It may be found parading the pond margins feeding on insects and their larvae.

COOT (*Fulica atra*)

The coot needs sufficiently deep water for feeding and will eat various aquatic weeds as well as molluscs and insect larvae. Dense bank-side vegetation is a key requirement for nesting and coots tend to be associated with larger ponds, as well as reservoirs and lakes. They are common and resident birds in all lowland parts of the British Isles.

CORMORANT (*Phalacrocorax carbo*)

Strictly speaking a marine species, but one that has recently begun to move to lowland inland waters across the British Isles as fish stocks around the coastline decline. Dedicated fish-eaters, cormorants need larger bodies of water in which to feed.

GADWALL (*Anas strepera*)

At a distance, the gadwall is an inconspicuous dabbling duck. On closer examination, the male's plumage is quite dashing. An introduced species, its British distribution is mainly concentrated to the more southern and eastern counties but it is spreading. Resident and shy, it needs good bank-side vegetation in which to nest.

GREAT CRESTED GREBE (*Podiceps cristatus*)

Almost brought to the brink of extinction in the British Isles by the Victorian millinery trade – its feathers were in demand – this large and elegant resident grebe is now once again reasonably common throughout lowland areas and on large expanses of still water. Fish are the principal prey and any pond will need to hold a substantial stock of small fish to support a pair of these extremely handsome birds. See colour section for illustration.

GREY HERON (*Ardea cinerea*)

This is largest of the European herons but it will visit even the smallest of garden ponds in search of frogs or fish. It hunts mainly in the marshy margins of the pond or in water shallow enough for it to wade. A resident species that can be found in most parts of the British Isles.

KINGFISHER (*Alcedo atthis*)

Our most brilliantly coloured resident bird is fairly widespread in southern and central England but less common further north, where colder winters restrict their expansion. Nesting takes place in tunnels excavated in banks, which may be at some distance from the water. Prey is largely small fish although insects are also taken. See colour section for illustration.

LITTLE GREBE (*Tachybaptus ruficollis*)

This small and attractive grebe can be found on still waters and slower-flowing rivers across the lowlands of the British Isles. It is a shy bird and will dive when disturbed, often re-surfacing at some distance from where last seen. It likes seclusion and needs good cover and a reasonably large area of water for breeding and hunting aquatic invertebrates. It is resident all year round.

MALLARD (*Anas platyrhynchos*)

Without doubt the most familiar of our resident ducks. It is highly adaptable and will populate relatively small ponds even where these are regularly disturbed by human activity. They are catholic in their diet and will eat seeds, plants, berries, insects and molluscs.

MOORHEN (*Gallinula chloropus*)

Abundant and widespread, the moorhen can be found on all but the smallest of ponds throughout the year. Although it generally nests in pond margins, it will readily feed on land – on a wide variety of vegetation, fruits, molluscs, worms and insects. Despite being found in built-up areas, it is a somewhat shy and retiring species; its harsh and penetrating call is often the only clue to its presence.

MUTE SWAN (*Cygnus olor*)

The mute swan is unmistakable and the largest bird species, by some margin, to reside on British inland waters. It needs a large area of water for feeding and nesting and is unlikely to be present on smaller ponds except in extreme circumstances. It can be found in most lowland areas and is present throughout the year.

REED BUNTING (*Emberiza schoeniclus*)

This handsome bunting can be found in a variety of habitats but is traditionally more associated with wetland. Ponds that have a good stand of reeds may attract the odd pair, providing there is a supply of insects and seeds. It is a resident species and can be found across much of the British Isles with the exception of the more mountainous regions.

REED WARBLER (*Acrocephalus scirpaceus*)

Reed warblers are likely to be found only in the densest reed beds and consequently only on larger ponds, reservoirs, lakes and estuaries. They are summer visitors mainly restricted to the south and east of England, and can be numerous in good habitat. Insects are taken during the spring and summer months and berries in autumn.

SEDGE WARBLER (*Acrocephalus schoenobaenus*)

These summer visitors are not exclusively associated with aquatic habitats, but they generally prefer to nest close to water and where there is good cover. They can be found in lowland counties of the British Isles. Insects are the main prey with autumn berries providing an additional supplement.

SNIPE (*Gallinago gallinago*)

Extremely cryptic in plumage and retiring in nature, this long-billed wader is a widespread but increasingly thinly distributed resident species whose numbers are augmented in winter by incoming Europeans. Birds visiting ponds require muddy areas in which to feed and a certain amount of cover in which to crouch down when roosting.

TEAL (*Anas crecca*)

Teal are small and very pretty dabbling ducks found in most regions of Britain; they are more common as a breeding bird in the north but tend to winter in southerly parts of the country. Being a shy species, they prefer waters that are well vegetated. They feed on invertebrates and seeds.

TUFTED DUCK (*Aythya fuligula*)

The tufted duck is a medium-sized diving species found across lowland Britain but becoming more common further east. Pairs can be found all year round on smaller ponds.

WATER RAIL (*Rallus aquaticus*)

Like other rails, this is a highly secretive species that will breed around smaller ponds with dense vegetation. Although resident, visiting birds from the European mainland swell numbers in winter. It is widespread but thinly distributed and more often heard than seen. Water rails have a wide diet and will take small fish, frogs and snails, as well as invertebrates. See colour section for illustration.

MAMMALS

Small ponds are unlikely to attract mammals on a regular basis, but larger ponds in the wider countryside can be important additional habitats for a wide range of mammalian species. While many mammals visit freshwater sites to drink and bathe, this chapter deals with the few native species that are directly associated with ponds.

BATS (*various species*)

Ponds attract flying insects, which in turn attract bats. The species described here are particularly associated with fresh water.

Daubenton's bat (*Myotis daubentonii*) is relatively common and widespread across the British Isles and hunts low over rivers, canals, lakes and larger ponds. It is a medium-sized bat. See colour section for illustration. The noctule bat (*Nyctalus noctula*) has a strong affinity with water. It can be found from the Scottish Borders southwards. It is relatively easy to recognise by its sleek form and large size. The whiskered bat (*Myotis mystacinus*) is widely distributed across southern Scotland, England, Wales and Northern Ireland. It occasionally feeds along watercourses.

See pages 89–90 for information on the law as it relates to the protection of species and habitats.

BROWN RAT (*Rattus norvegicus*)

The brown rat prefers damp and watery situations and is a strong swimmer – it is also a serious pest. Where large populations are present, the risk of contracting Weil's disease –

introduced into the water through the animal's urine – is a serious issue. Infection occurs when open sores and wounds come into contact with contaminated pond water.

EUROPEAN BEAVER (*Castor fiber*)

Once a common British resident, the beaver was hunted to extinction in recent historical times. It is mentioned here as there are now small populations being re-introduced under licence into parts of England and Scotland – some of these sites are larger ponds and gravel pits rather than rivers, which are this animal's natural home.

OTTER (*Lutra lutra*)

Predominantly an animal of coasts and river systems, the otter will on occasion visit larger ponds within its hunting territories in search of food. During the 20th century the otter was eradicated from much of its habitat, but is now regaining ground as river quality and bank-sides improve – and through the help of conservation societies. While not thought of kindly by some fishermen (due to their diet), otters can play a valuable role in fishery management as they tend to push out mink populations. (Mink can cause considerably more damage to fish stocks than a pair of otters will.) Otters will also eat alien red signal crayfish – to the benefit of our remaining native crayfish populations. Eels are their favoured prey species. See colour section for illustration.

In spite of a welcome improvement in the otter's fortunes, many still die on our roads and through drowning in eel traps. See pages 89–90 for information on the law as it relates to the protection of species and habitats.

WATER SHREW (*Neomys fodiens*)

Present throughout mainland Britain, this species is the largest of the European shrews. It feeds on small fish, frogs and insects, and it can dive and swim in pursuit of its prey.

WATER VOLE (*Arvicola terrestris*)

The water vole has a special place in our hearts, in large part thanks to Kenneth Grahame's *Wind in the Willows,* in which Ratty (the loveable water vole) plays a principal role. Despite our affection for this charming little semi-aquatic animal, it has suffered a decline in the British Isles. Water pollution, the canalisation of rivers, the removal of bank-side vegetation, competition from the alien American mink, the ingestion of rodenticides and the infilling of larger ponds in the landscape have all contributed to a catastrophic reduction in numbers. Despite much effort by conservation bodies, populations still seem to be falling. This is not helped by the fact that water voles rarely survive the first six months of their lives and those that do almost never get beyond a second winter.

Mating activity persists throughout the spring and summer months and up to eight young may be raised in one litter. Water voles burrow into the soft banks of suitable water bodies, including ponds where these are a reasonable size. They survive on a diet of plant materials. Population densities are generally low in any one area and individual territories are marked by scent and vigorously defended against other water voles. They are excellent swimmers and are often spotted as they make their way in the shallows along the water bank.

See pages 89–90 for information on the law as it relates to the protection of species and habitats.

ALIEN SPECIES

A variety of plants and animals have been deliberately introduced into the British Isles over the years and some of them have had an impact on lakes, rivers and ponds. Many are most unwelcome additions to our flora and fauna and serious efforts should be made to remove and destroy them. Not to do so risks alien species displacing natives through competition and, in the case of animals, predation, inter-breeding and spread of disease. Introducing alien species into the wild is highly irresponsible and illegal.

ALIEN PLANTS

Plants have often been introduced into the wild unwittingly. Negligent stockists may offer unsuitable and occasionally illegal species to an unsuspecting public. Even indigenous plants bought from less-than-reputable suppliers can harbour viable fragments of invasive or illegal plant matter in the soil of the purchased plant. (The eggs of undesirable water creatures and various pathogens can also accompany such purchases.) To avoid risks it is best to source plants from suppliers who guarantee that their stocks are exclusively native but not taken from the wild.

Once alien plants are established in a garden pond they can spread to the wild by all the usual means – birds and animals carrying off seeds, fragments and so on.

The following (alphabetically ordered) plant list comprises species that may be improperly offered for sale and which are alien and highly invasive. These should therefore be excluded from any planting list. Where they are already present then urgent action should be taken to eradicate them – in some cases this will require the professional application of herbicides.

Canadian pondweed (*Elodea canadensis*)
Curly waterweed (*Lagarosiphon major*)
Fairy fern (*Azolla filiculoides*)
Fanwort (*Cabomba caroliniana*)
Floating pennywort (*Hydrocotyle ranunculoides*)
Giant salvinia (*Salvinia molesta*)
Green seafingers (*Codium fragile*)
Himalayan balsam (*Impatiens glandulifera*)
Least duckweed (*Lemna minuta*)
New Zealand pigmyweed (*Crassula helmsii*)
New Zealand swamp-stonecrop (*Crassula helmsii*)
Nuttall's pondweed (*Elodea nuttallii*)
Parrot's-feather (*Myriophyllum aquaticum*)
Water fern (*Azolla filiculoides*)
Water hyacinth (*Eichhornia crassipes*)
Water lettuce (*Pistia stratiotes*)
Water primrose (*Ludwigia grandiflora*)

ALIEN ANIMALS

Alien amphibians and reptiles are unlikely to be introduced by accident except where breeding stocks (from scientific establishments and the like) escape into the wider environment. Where this happens, or where deliberate release occurs, the effect on the indigenous amphibian and reptile populations can be devastating – through competition, aggression or the spread of disease.

Some introduced species do seem to have found a vacant niche in this island's biodiversity and apparently cause no harm; but that doesn't mean you should consider adding them to your pond unless it is done under licence and as part of a controlled programme.

Other animals that have no place in this country and that have caused and continue to cause significant problems for our native wildlife are thankfully few and far between. However, there are two species that are extremely problematic, common and widespread in still waters and waterways across large swathes of the British Isles: the American mink and the red signal crayfish (see page 47). These should be removed, under licence, wherever possible. Catching crayfish, using baited traps, has the added bonus of providing the basis of a fine meal.

The following list details those exotic species that have either been the subject of various illegal releases or pose the greatest risk to indigenous animals.

AMERICA MINK (*Mustela vison*)

The American mink is an unwanted escapee from fur farms, its existence in the wild often the result of deliberate action by animal liberationists. It is now widespread in most open habitats and there is barely an inland water body that it hasn't colonised. See below and colour section for illustration. The mink is a powerful predator and a good swimmer and will take a wide variety of prey, including fish, mammals, birds, amphibians and reptiles. The spread of the mink is a major cause of the demise of our native water vole. Trapping can and should be carried out (under licence and taking appropriate care to ensure other animals are not mistakenly caught and damaged) on a regular basis and the animals humanely destroyed.

AFRICAN CLAWED TOAD (*Xenopus laevis*)

Mainly a scientific laboratory escapee that has not, as yet, been recorded as having bred in the British Isles. The south of Wales and the Isle of Wight are the main areas where the toads have been sighted. Like the bull frog (below), we must hope that this species does not become established as its large size and appetite present a threat to our smaller native wildlife.

ALPINE NEWT (*Triturus alpestris*)

Believed to be reasonably widespread, in England at least, the alpine newt is an escapee from captivity. It is a small newt and, perhaps thankfully, remains uncommon.

BULL FROG (*Lithobates catesbeianus*)

This American brute is one of the most unfortunate of all introductions to the British countryside as far as our native wildlife is concerned. The pet trade can take much responsibility here for the ready sale of bull-frog tadpoles. The bull frog is a voracious and formidable predator of smaller creatures, and it is vital that any populations are destroyed and the animal eradicated from these shores. Present in a few locations largely in the south-east of England.

EDIBLE FROG (*Pelophylax esculentus*)

The edible frog is a peculiar creature, being the fertile hybrid offspring of cross-bred pool frogs (a rare but possibly native species – see Amphibians and Reptiles, page 69) and marsh frogs (see below). It is difficult to determine whether edible frogs were introduced to the British Isles or whether populations have sprung up where the two species have interbred. Populations exist in south-east England and East Anglia, and the species is poised to continue its spread. Breeding is in late spring/early summer and the edible frog also calls loudly at this time.

ITALIAN CRESTED NEWT (*Triturus carnifex*)

It is thought that this European import has established itself in a few discrete locations in southern England after escaping from captive populations, rather than having been deliberately released. It is unfortunate that the Italian crested newt has found a home here as it interbreeds with our native great crested newt, which is a threatened species.

MARSH FROG (*Pelophylax ridibundus*)

Introduced to Romney Marsh in the 1930s, this species has gone on to conquer much of Sussex and Kent. It occurs in other southern counties, where it has been introduced, and seems set to continue its spread. It's a large green frog and calls loudly in the breeding season in late spring. Tadpoles may overwinter in breeding ponds and emerge as adults the following spring.

MIDWIFE TOAD (*Alytes obstetricans*)

This introduction seems not to present a significant threat to native wildlife. Colonies persist in the vicinity of the original release sites in the Midlands and South Devon, but they do not appear to have significantly expanded their populations or distribution. Smaller in size than our indigenous toads and grey in colour, the midwife toad has a liking for small ponds in which to breed and is nocturnal.

RED SIGNAL CRAYFISH (*Pacifastacus leniusculus*)

In places illegally or unintentionally introduced or where it has escaped from commercial farms, this crayfish will quickly colonise larger ponds as well as rivers, canals and streams. This relative of the lobster has been largely responsible for helping bring about the demise of our only native freshwater crayfish, the white-clawed crayfish (*Austropotamobius pallipes* – see page 47), a now uncommon resident of clean, fresh waters. The larger American species both out-competes and has spread fungal disease to its native cousin.

TERRAPINS (*various species*)

North American terrapins have occasionally been released into still waters and rivers in Britain, particularly into town and city ponds. While these have proved to be capable of growing to full size, it is unlikely (even with the advance of global warming) that conditions will be suitable for them to form viable breeding populations. However, they are voracious eaters and adult animals can take prey as large as ducklings. Where present they should be removed by the appropriate authorities.

LAW, SAFETY AND GOOD PRACTICE

As with most pursuits, pastimes and activities, the enjoyment that comes with creating, owning, maintaining and using a pond is accompanied by a necessary set of obligations and responsibilities. Many of these are enshrined in law, at some level, and all are concerned with the wellbeing and protection of life – be it human, animal or plant. However, even where legislation does not demand it, good practice (in regard to the care of the environment and that which depends on it) is desirable and should provide improved results and greater satisfaction for those involved in caring for ponds.

THE LAW

When creating and managing ponds, care should be taken to observe local, national, European and international law in regard to the protection of various species and habitats.

It can be both illegal and undesirable to either remove plant material and/or animals (and their eggs) from a wild source or introduce plant material and/or animals (and their eggs) to a habitat. Indigenous wildlife will generally and eventually find its own way into a (new) pond where populations exist nearby. Attempting to accelerate this process through removing specimens, eggs or spawn from other wild sources, for the purposes of stocking a (new) pond, can place the originating population at risk and introduce disease to the pond where the plants or animals are imported. Introducing invasive or alien plants and animals to a habitat (pond) can be damaging to the environment at large and is illegal.

Ponds, in themselves, are not directly protected by legislation. However, some ponds have specific protection where they are of international importance. Ponds can also be placed under the protection of law where they are considered to have sufficient habitat value or significance. Ponds that support protected species will have various levels of protection as relevant to those protected species present. It can be an offence to interfere, in any way, with the animals themselves or the habitat in which they exist.

The release of any fish into ponds or other water bodies is strictly governed by appropriate consents, except where the pond is in a garden and has no outlet to any natural water bodies and, where necessary, sufficient precautions have been taken suitable to prevent the escape of introduced fish into the natural environment.

PLANNING PERMISSION

Planning permission may be required where:
- there is a 'change of use' of the land (for example, from agricultural use to nature conservation or recreation);
- engineering operations need to be undertaken (especially where such may interfere with drains, subterranean cables and pipes and other such utilities);
- the construction of the pond may have adverse affects on highways or neighbouring properties;
- the construction of the pond may affect the natural purpose of floodplains;
- the construction of the pond may affect important wildlife, wildlife habitats and/or archaeological sites;
- the pond is close to an airport or helipad.

See your local council authority website for more information.

SAFETY

DROWNING

Wherever there is a risk of human drowning, all reasonable precautions should be taken to reduce such risk. This is especially important where children are likely to come into contact with water. Consider whether fencing, plantings or other barriers should be provided to prevent access to the water – especially where public land, highways, rights of way or permitted paths border any part of the pond. (Such precautions may be necessary, in law and/or to meet required planning consents and insurances, where the public may be placed at any risk).

Consider whether life rings should be made available and be made sufficiently visible and accessible. (Again such provision may be required necessary, in law and/or to meet required planning consents and insurances, where the public may be placed at any risk).

When wading in (deep) water the wader should ensure that another able person is present and that a rope connects both partners (or is attached to the wader and to a secure point on the bank). Consider also the use of lifejackets or other suitable inflatable life aids.

DISEASE

The issue of disease must be considered both in terms of the pond user contracting disease from contact with the water and the pond user spreading disease to a pond. In the case of the former, contact with pond water should be avoided where the pond user has any open sores, wounds or abrasions. The use of barrier creams and gloves may be considered prudent even where the user has no evidence of broken skin. The most potentially serious disease contracted through pond water coming into contact with open sores is Weil's disease. While this is comparatively rare in the UK there is a significant risk especially where brown rats are present as they can contaminate water bodies through their urine.

The spread of pathogens by human agency can be reduced or eliminated by good hygiene practice. At its most simple this means thoroughly cleaning (with a suitable disinfectant) all footwear, waders and other equipment (including fishing tackle) before bringing them into contact with the pond.

ELECTROCUTION

Take extreme care and follow all manufacturers' instructions when installing electrical pumps, fountains or other such water features. Ensure that there is a power-breaker (or other appropriate circuit-breaking device) between the main power source and the device. Ensure all cabling is sufficiently protected (by armoured casing) from damage and adequately marked especially where the cable is buried and where there is a risk of cutting through the cable by digging and so on. Do not use electrical power tools in the vicinity of ponds.

Where overhead power lines are present ensure that these are shielded, where possible, and provide adequate warnings of the danger of electrocution (especially where power lines are situated close to ponds that are used for fishing and where carbon-fibre rods and/or wet lines may come into contact with live wires).

FURTHER READING

Collins Guide to Freshwater Fishes of Britain and Europe Bent J Muus & Preben Dahlstrom, William Collins, 1967

The New Atlas of Breeding Birds in Britain and Ireland: 1988–1991, David Wingfield Gibbons & James B Reid & Robert A Chapman, T & AD Poyser, 1993

Fauna Britannica, Stefan Buczacki, Hamlyn, 2002

Cassell's Wild Flowers of Britain and Northern Europe, Marjory Blamey & Christopher Grey-Wilson, Cassell, 2003

Creating Small Habitats for Wildlife in your Garden, Josie Briggs, Guild of Master Craftsmen, 2000

The Pond Book: A Guide to the Management and Creation of Ponds, P Williams, J Biggs, M Whitfield, A Thorne, S Bryant, G Fox & P Nicolet, Pond Conservations Trust, 1999

Amphibians and Reptiles: A Natural History of British Herpetofauna, Trevor Beebee & Richard Griffiths, HarperCollins, 2000

British Bats, John D Altringham, HarperCollins, 2003

Collins Field Guide to Freshwater Life, Richard Fitter & Richard Manuel, William Collins, 1986

Flora Britannica, Richard Mabey, Chatto & Windus, 1997

ORGANISATIONS

British Dragonfly Society
www.dragonflysoc.org.uk

The British Herpetological Society
www.thebhs.org

The British Trust for Ornithology
www.bto.org

The Environment Agency
www.environment-agency.gov.uk

Froglife
www.froglife.org

The Mammal Society
www.abdn.ac.uk/mammal

The Herpetological
Conservation Trust
www.herpconstrust.org.uk

The National Trust
www.nationaltrust.org.uk

National Trust for Scotland
www.nts.org.uk

Natural England
www.naturalengland.org.uk

Pond Conservation Trust
www.pondconservation.org.uk

The Royal Society for the
Protection of Birds
www.rspb.org.uk

Scottish Wildlife Trust
www.swt.org.uk

The Wildfowl and
Wetlands Trust
www.wwt.org.uk

The Wildlife Trusts
www.wildlifetrusts.org

USEFUL WEBSITES

Conservation Natural Habitats
Regulations 1994
www.opsi.gov.uk

The Countryside and Rights of
Way Act 2000
www.opsi.gov.uk

The Department of Food
and Rural Affairs
www.defra.gov.uk

Environment Agency
www.environment-agency.gov.uk

European Habitats Directive
(Annex I)
www.jncc.gov.uk

Local Biodiversity Action Plans
(see also local council authority
websites)
www.ukbap.org.uk

Natural England
www.naturalengland.org.uk

Natural Environment and Rural
Communities Act 2006
www.defra.gov.uk

The Northern Ireland
Environment Agency
www.ni-environment.gov.uk

Scottish Environment
Protection Agency
www.sepa.org.uk

The Scottish Government
www.scotland.gov.uk

Wildlife and Countryside Act 1981
www.jncc.gov.uk

INDEX